# RESEARCHING CHILDREN AND CHILDHOODS

ALSO AVAILABLE FROM BLOOMSBURY

*Writing a Watertight Thesis*, Mike Bottery, Nigel Wright and Mark A. Fabrizi

*Research Methods for Understanding Professional Learning*, Elaine Hall and Kate Wall

*Reflective Teaching in Higher Education*, Paul Ashwin with David Boud, Susanna Calkins, Kelly Coate, Fiona Hallett, Grey Light, Kathy Luckett, Jan McArthur, Iain McLaren, Monica McLean, Velda McCune, Katarina Mårtensson and Michelle Tooher

*Using Questions to Think*, Nathan Eric Dickman

*Narrative Inquiry*, Vera Caine, D. Jean Clandinin and Sean Lessard

*Embodied Inquiry*, Jennifer Leigh and Nicole Brown

*Diary Method*, Ruth Bartlett and Christine Milligan

*Community Studies*, Graham Crow

*Inclusive Research*, Melanie Nind

# RESEARCHING CHILDREN AND CHILDHOODS

*A Reflexive Dissertation Companion*

## SARAH RICHARDS AND SARAH COOMBS

BLOOMSBURY ACADEMIC
LONDON • NEW YORK • OXFORD • NEW DELHI • SYDNEY

BLOOMSBURY ACADEMIC
Bloomsbury Publishing Plc
50 Bedford Square, London, WC1B 3DP, UK
1385 Broadway, New York, NY 10018, USA
29 Earlsfort Terrace, Dublin 2, Ireland

BLOOMSBURY, BLOOMSBURY ACADEMIC and the Diana logo
are trademarks of Bloomsbury Publishing Plc

First published in Great Britain 2025

Copyright © Sarah Richards and Sarah Coombs, 2025

Sarah Richards and Sarah Coombs have asserted their right under the Copyright, Designs and Patents Act, 1988, to be identified as Authors of this work.

For legal purposes the Acknowledgements on p. viii constitute an extension of this copyright page.

Cover design by Catherine Wood
Cover image © BOULENGER Xavier/Shutterstock

All rights reserved. No part of this publication may be reproduced or transmitted in any form or by any means, electronic or mechanical, including photocopying, recording, or any information storage or retrieval system, without prior permission in writing from the publishers.

Bloomsbury Publishing Plc does not have any control over, or responsibility for, any third-party websites referred to or in this book. All internet addresses given in this book were correct at the time of going to press. The author and publisher regret any inconvenience caused if addresses have changed or sites have ceased to exist, but can accept no responsibility for any such changes.

A catalogue record for this book is available from the British Library.

Library of Congress Control Number: 2025932363

ISBN: HB: 978-1-3500-4321-3
PB: 978-1-3500-4320-6
ePDF: 978-1-3500-4323-7
eBook: 978-1-3500-4322-0

Typeset by Integra Software Services Pvt. Ltd.
Printed and bound in Great Britain

To find out more about our authors and books visit www.bloomsbury.com and sign up for our newsletters.

*This volume is dedicated to all our students past and present, whose questions and experiences in their research were the genesis of this book. We hope the content that these students inspired assists future students on their research journey.*

# CONTENTS

*Acknowledgements* viii

Introduction 1

1 Engaging with Ethics 13

2 Navigating the Methodological Maze 39

3 Considering Child-Centred Research 57

4 Utilizing Key Concepts 75

5 Worrying That 'I've Got No Data' 101

6 Putting 'I' into Research with Children 119

*References* 140
*Index* 149

# ACKNOWLEDGEMENTS

We would like to express our gratitude to Professor Heather Montgomery for her kind permission to include excerpts from her seminal research with children in Thailand.

# Introduction

To begin, let us introduce ourselves as the authors of this volume. For many years we, that is quite confusingly, Sarah and Sarah, have supervised undergraduate, postgraduate and PhD students in the completion of their research projects. The dissertation process, from the first supervision meeting to the final submission of the document, can perhaps be likened to a rollercoaster, containing highs and lows, periods of struggle and times of great enjoyment. Despite or perhaps because of such variation, working with students across the entirety of this research journey is a privilege, and one in which both student and supervisor learn a great deal, not only about the topics being explored and the nature of research with children but also about themselves.

It is with such experiences in mind, plus all the students we have supervised over the years, that the rationale for writing this volume became clear. It is our hope that this volume acts as a companion to undergraduate and postgraduate students who are about to embark on qualitative, primary research projects with children. Rather than act as a 'how to' guide, of which there are many, the purpose of this book is to highlight opportunities for you to engage in critical research debates throughout your dissertation. To support you in this undertaking, we present relevant topics, concepts and perspectives, all of which are highly pertinent to research with children and provide ample opportunities for critical discussions and deeper interrogation. Equally, a variety of research examples, all of which we have encountered personally, either in our own research or in that of our supervisees, are included throughout the chapters to help provide realistic and contextual details, and moments for thought and reflection.

We acknowledge that a research project can be daunting for anyone, from those for whom it is their daily occupation, to those who face its challenges less frequently, and perhaps most especially for students who have not encountered its complexities before. As a student, the process of producing a dissertation, may seem fraught with worries, tensions and uncertainties. Yet, each year students overcome such concerns and submit insightful projects that demonstrate their care and consideration of young participants, their knowledge and understanding of a chosen topic area, and their creative, critical and theoretically grounded approach to research.

From the outset, you may doubt your ability to produce this large and seemingly complex document and you may have a bewildering number of questions that require answers; what topic to explore; how to go about gaining ethical approval; which methods to select; where to find participants; how to analyse data; and many more. Even if you are quite confident about your topic choice and how you want to proceed in gaining your data, the early stages of a dissertation can be a perplexing time. At this point, when the possibilities are endless, but time is pressing, students may feel encouraged to adopt an initially less time-consuming, and seemingly more straightforward approach to their project, such as a systematic review. Thus avoiding the perceived complications and obstacles, often associated with research with children; for example, gaining access to participants, the deliberations of ethics panels, the writing of appropriate information and consent letters and so on. However, it is our hope that this volume, and the research stories in it, will encourage those who are in a position to carry out research with children to embrace this opportunity. Not only will it provide you with memorable fieldwork and develop your understanding of the research process, but it will enrich your dissertation through the exploration of both established and emerging research concepts. For example, when conducting primary research with children, the ethical approval process encourages student researchers to emphasize the agentic child in their research design, and yet, the ethics documentation prioritizes principles of protection and welfarism, thus constructing an image of the vulnerable child (Richards, Clark and Boggis 2015). This contradiction, though rarely interrogated by students, offers opportunities for critical evaluation of key themes in research with children, such as power, research relationships and canonical narratives of childhood itself.

Demonstrating knowledge and understanding of the research process and offering critical insights into key arguments relevant to research with children are the key drivers of your dissertation. Nevertheless, students tend to focus on what they find, or worry about what they do not find, and yet this is not your dissertation's whole reason for being. We contend that the richness of qualitative, participatory approaches is that the process of doing research can be as central as the research topic itself. Therefore, your discussions within the dissertation can, and perhaps should, include reflexive accounts of how you engaged with your topic; your chosen method; your interactions with your participants and the relationships you developed with them; the ethical dilemmas that emerged; as well as how you as an individual shaped the knowledge you constructed. These relational conversations and explorations provide abundant opportunities for critical evaluation throughout your dissertation, offer valuable lessons in doing research with children and position you as a subjective individual in your own research endeavour.

We now select and further develop some of these conversations as we highlight the content and main themes of the chapters you will encounter in this volume. Each chapter begins by introducing key ideas and contemporary concepts relevant to research with children, with perhaps some of the more contentious debates, such as those surrounding the presence of the first-person pronoun. If you have already taken a glance through the chapters, you might have noticed the presence of activity boxes scattered throughout. Our intention for these is diverse. On occasion, they are intended to help you build content such as your methodology. Some activities aim to set out key ethical concepts. Others perhaps, encourage you to recognize your positionality in your research or inspire your critical reflection on key themes. Engaging with these activities is advantageous, making some of the more complex concepts and methodological debates appear less abstract or remote. Likewise, your responses to the activities can help you to construct sections of your dissertation, thus, more effectively, demonstrating your critical knowledge and understanding. Many of these activities have been drawn from our experiences of supervising student dissertations, whereby engaging with such encourages students to apply multifaceted research themes and debates to their dissertations.

# Chapter 1 Engaging with Ethics

It is not by mistake that we begin this volume with a discussion of ethics. For so long viewed as merely an initial stepping stone from which to begin your research, this chapter considers ethics to be the foundation on which your dissertation is built, and fundamental to research with children. The main emphasis of this chapter therefore concentrates on ethics, not just as a procedural hoop to be jumped through, although we will examine this aspect of it, but rather as a way of thinking and behaving. Thus, throughout your dissertation, engagement with ethical discussions can provide fruitful opportunities for critical consideration. Take, for example, the procedural elements of ethics, we may not always value them, but they so often support us in producing ethical research projects. Consider also how the ethical principles and practices you adopt during your research are influenced by your own personal attitudes and beliefs about children and their childhoods. Taking time to contemplate these wider ethical debates brings ethics into proximity with the self, yourself. What might have previously been construed as intangible concepts become reflections of yourself as an individual and a researcher, and thereby the mainstay of your dissertation narrative and reflexive account.

Understandably, the chapter begins by exploring the procedural elements of gaining ethical approval. Chronologically this is often the first context in which students are asked to engage with, and begin, their ethical journey. It can be an anxious time in which to first encounter ethics, as focus often dictates that exploration of ideas is limited to writing proposals, completing forms, providing letters of information for participants and nervously awaiting the outcome of a university ethics panel. From this position, ethics can become a tick-box exercise to be completed, and subsequently perhaps even forgotten. However, our intention is not to suggest that ethics is done and dusted as soon as the ethics panel has deliberated, but rather to extend our thinking beyond procedures and illustrate opportunities for ethical discussion throughout the entirety of your work.

With the above aim in mind, we have constructed this chapter to cover the following key features of ethics in research with children. First, we anticipate that this chapter supports the development of your own personal ethical narrative, where situating ethical principles and practices are central tenets. Second, the chapter presents information and debates that encourage you to be ethical, not just in your application for an ethics committee but in moments and decisions throughout your research where only you see your actions. Ultimately, our aim is for you to recognize yourself as an ethical researcher in both principle and practice, where you are inextricable from the decisions you make and the actions you take.

# Chapter 2 Navigating the Methodological Maze

Notwithstanding the prioritization of ethical discussions in this volume, you would equally need to identify some of your own methodological values in order to recognize, and begin to assemble, the ethical principles that should inform your research. In other words, methodology and ethics are inextricably linked. For example, the position and extent to which children will be participating in your study are methodological decisions, which have particular ethical implications. Methodology is often considered a tricky concept by students, who can sometimes suggest that they do not understand what a methodology is and are unsure of the differences between it and their method. As a result, methodology can sometimes be neglected by students to the detriment of their work. However, in a similar way to our approach to ethics, considered in the previous chapter, our intention for this chapter is that students begin to realize that the methodological and/or philosophical stance they take is a manifestation of themselves. Each of us, as researchers, is embedded in our research, across every section and in every interpretation.

In this context a methodological approach includes your personal values, beliefs and principles in relation to childhood and children's lives. For example, if you believe that children should have their voices heard then one of your methodological values should be the centrality of voice. Therefore, you will focus on the promotion of those voices to the forefront of your discussions. In this chapter you will find activities that encourage you to recognize your personal values and assumptions about childhood, and these then help you to identify the principles that become the building blocks of your methodology.

Underpinning participatory research with children are fundamental principles related to qualitative research more generally. These include concepts such as interpretivism and sometimes key theoretical ideas drawn from feminism, such as subjectivity, positionality, reflexivity and an ethic of care. This chapter will explain these concepts and help you to build your own personal methodological approach, which ultimately privileges your ideas around children and their involvement in research. Developing a methodological stance for your project is therefore a creative and personal process, which cannot simply be taken off the shelf and made applicable. Therefore, you get to select the components as you would with sweets in a pick-n-mix bag. In this way the methodology is not only unique to you, but it also reveals you.

# Chapter 3 Considering Child-Centred Research

This next chapter engages with how changing scientific and societal beliefs led to the emergence of 'new' approaches to participatory research with children. Children's involvement in research has changed significantly from previously dominant positivist approaches, which were primarily done unto children, to more qualitative methods conducted with children. The manifestation of children's rights and the central notions of voice, participation and agency, became, and often remain, monoliths in this type of research. Yet, this volume offers you critical and questioning approaches to these often-immutable standpoints. Thereby, providing the circumstances for you to develop analytical debates in your own research project.

Such recent principles of agency, voice and participation as key components of the child-focused turn have been celebrated and championed by childhood scholars. However, initially these concepts lacked interrogation until more recently. Therefore, in this chapter we outline the development of child-focused research and include critical evaluation of these key concepts in order to enable you to not only apply but also evaluate these fundamental notions. Furthermore, we encourage you to situate your research with children into the social contexts in which children live their lives and in which you gathered your data. Again, this can often be a neglected feature of research discussions, and by omission reduces the richness and contextual nature that ultimately shapes children's participation, agency and voice.

## Chapter 4 Utilizing Key Concepts

This chapter introduces several exciting, rewarding but sometimes neglected concepts, such as positionality, self-disclosure, category entitlement, subjectivity and reflexivity. The aim of this chapter is to make these positions more accessible to you via explanation, clarification and examples. The chapter will take each concept in turn, beginning with subjectivity and reflexivity, in order to provide deeper insights into its origins and purpose. Furthermore, we consider their application and evaluation in your study. Here we encourage you to consider applying these ideas to your dissertation and thus enable critical discussion of the research process. A significant rationale for the presence of these concepts in your dissertation is to demonstrate your understanding of their relevance and importance to the construction and analysis of your data. By the application of these ideas, your role and the ways you have shaped your research become evident. These concepts enable you to recognize yourself or your many selves within your topic, methodology, analysis and throughout your dissertation. Who you are shapes what you find, how you find it and what you say about it.

## Chapter 5 Worrying That 'I've Got No Data'

The focus of this chapter evolved from our experiences of students returning from their fieldwork and worriedly announcing that they have no data, and some in fact claiming that they have nothing at all, as everything went horribly wrong. In a similar way to our supervision sessions over the years we suggest that this is very rarely the case. Therefore, the aim of this chapter is not only to offer you reassurances but to help you develop valuable conversations in relation to the planning and collecting of your data. Furthermore, to encourage you to recognize that you do indeed have data, even if it is not quite what you expected.

As students of childhood studies, and in particular students who are about to embark on research with children, you are likely to have encountered that children often have their own agendas. The research process is no different, and it is often this unpredictability that draws us to the excitement of researching with children. Utilizing examples from previous research by both us and our students we encourage you to identify your own preconceived assumptions about your data, outline how to manage unexpected data and how to recognize the data you have. What children say can sometimes be disconcerting, how to respond to unanticipated claims, disclosures and silences is also explored here. As a final theme of this chapter, we explore how we can, as researchers, often find ourselves attached to data, often not integral to the claims and discussions we make. We therefore suggest the possibility of including this extraneous data, rather than leaving it on the cutting room floor.

# Chapter 6 Putting 'I' into Research with Children

In a similar way to previous chapters, which have aided you in creating your own methodological approach, ethical account and reflexive explanations of your positionality and category entitlements, this final chapter aims to help you uncover and employ your own narrative voice. Scholars have long regarded the use of the first-person pronoun in academic writing as contentious due to the privileging of objectivity. Yet, this volume predominantly argues that researchers are inseparable from their work, and therefore attempting to eradicate ourselves from our own research projects is highly problematic.

To begin, the chapter outlines prevailing arguments for the exclusion of self and the subsequent suggestion that absence leads to a powerful, anonymous and neutral voice. However, even when academic protocols call for the removal of the researcher from their written accounts and insist on the use of third-person pronouns, researchers often, purposefully or not, retain their visibility. Notwithstanding these arguments of objectivity and detachment, the chapter goes on to consider the inclusion of the first-person pronoun, and its own authoritative nature. Several activities are provided to highlight the many ways in which writers position themselves in their texts, and how you might begin to recognize and potentially emulate these. As you will see, not all authors use the word 'I', rather through their choice of topic, their selection and inclusion of other authors voices, their methodological approach and/or the voices of their participants, their personal qualities are divulged.

Please note that the use of the first-person pronoun may not be an acceptable academic convention in your discipline. We suggest that you always seek your supervisor's guidance in this matter.

Our intention for this volume, has been to include a diverse, yet focused, range of debates and arguments, which should prove valuable in helping you to construct critical arguments in and throughout your dissertation. Notwithstanding such variety, from exploring ethical practices and methodological values, to considerations of children's agency, voice and participation, one commonality becomes evident across these disparate themes. Despite the centrality of some of these seemingly abstract notions, one recurring, yet implicit theme, is your presence. During your time as a university student, you are likely to have been told on numerous occasions, to be objective, to be unbiased and to remove any vestiges of self from your work. If not, your very presence risks contaminating it. Such stances encourage an absence from your research. Here we rather privilege your presence and show you ways to acknowledge self. This volume contends that removal of self is not possible and furthermore that presence should be recognized as a strength, through a critical and reflexive discussion. Acknowledging who you are in research and the many parts you play, from your choice of methodological underpinnings to the practical decisions you make, are not something to hide away from but rather something to be critically conceded and brought to the forefront of your dissertation. Therefore, all aspects of your study will ultimately mirror who you are.

Overall, this volume has generally encompassed qualitative, interpretative and feminist ideals with all their attendant qualities of care, reciprocity and relationships. We argue that adopting this methodological stance enables us to acknowledge our own sensitivities, the positions we bring to the field and the unavoidable emotional labour of doing research with children. However, we regard these as insightful tools to construct our research discussions. We do this through being continuously and critically reflexive of our approach, our findings and ourselves. Our aim for this volume was to help you construct sections of your dissertation, and also to encourage the articulation of your voice as a strength and presence. Ultimately, our intention was to provide you with the tools and debates that can elevate sections of your research into critically evaluative accounts that better demonstrate your knowledge and understanding of the research process and your role in it.

Finally, before we move on to engage with the central themes of this volume, we would like to wish you every success with your dissertation and trust that we can be of assistance through the pages of this volume. A dissertation might be considered a document of life (Plummer 2001) and/or a rite of passage. Undergraduate and postgraduate dissertations sit on our bookshelves gathering dust (perhaps now more often on our hard-drives) only to be opened from time-to-time to amaze ourselves at how clever we were then. The whole dissertation process, from voicing our initial ideas to submitting the finished product, has become the stuff of legend. The baton is passed to each new generation of students, accompanied by a collection of fabulous narratives that fan the flames of apprehension but ultimately speak of success. A completed dissertation is an accomplishment, a culmination of years of hard work and the realization of graduation. Overall, it is a success story, and we wish you every success with yours.

# 1
# Engaging with Ethics

## Introduction

The rationale for situating a chapter on ethics at the very start of this volume is to emphasize its absolute and fundamental importance to participatory research with children, and therefore, to your dissertation. As you embark on your own research project, we aspire to support you in developing your own ethical narrative that can underpin your study from its inception to the concluding remarks. The purpose of this chapter, therefore, is to situate ethics, ethical thinking and ethical practice as central threads that run throughout your work and assert their place at the forefront of your student research dissertation.

From the student perspective, ethical attention tends to fixate on the day of the university ethics panel, with its powers to approve, or not, your proposed dissertation. Once this early obstacle is successfully overcome, further ethical discussions have a propensity to be relegated to one prescribed section of the dissertation and limited to descriptions of the traditional rules and guidelines that so often dominate ethical debates in research with children; informed consent, confidentiality and anonymity, rights to withdraw and so on. Whilst these discussions are useful, the aim of this chapter is to draw your attention to wider ethical possibilities and provide you with greater opportunities to interrogate ethical issues. Here, we explore both ethical procedures and practices, and in this way elevate your ethical content from the confines of one section to a recurring theme throughout your study. Ethical conversations can range across the whole dissertation, from topic choice and participant selection to the importance of research-context, in-the-moment decision-making and the significance of your methodological preferences. To act as points of reflection, the chapter will also include some of our own 'cautionary tales', mainly in the form of vignettes. These illustrations are drawn from our wide-ranging experience as dissertation supervisors but also as researchers ourselves. We hope that these examples will illustrate some of the often-unexpected challenges and pitfalls that 'being ethical' can pose and thus encourage us, as researchers of childhood, to be more ethically reflexive.

## What Is Meant by Ethics?

Ethics is a wide-ranging and fluid concept, it is relative across time, cultures and contexts, and consequently can mean a multiplicity of things to a diversity of people. We might consider that the origins of ethics and ethical thinking began with basic notions of right and wrong, evolved through the complexities of moral philosophy, and subsequently developed into the ethical standards, procedures and practices we know today. Activity 1.1 should help you highlight what ethics means to you. At this early stage, we ask you to explore the concept of ethics from a broad perspective in relation to your everyday life.

---

**ACTIVITY 1.1**
Consider the following questions.
- What do you understand by the term *ethics?*
- What do you think it means to be *ethical or unethical?*

---

Engaging in this activity can reveal the relationship between ethical and moral behaviour and highlight the personal and relative nature of both ethics and morality. Unfortunately, the history of being ethical in research is littered with problems, and often a pronounced lack of ethical/moral engagement on the part of previous researchers. For instance, you may have heard of the [in]famous research studies of Stanley Milgram, conducted in the 1960s, and focused on obedience to authority, or the Untreated Syphilis Study at Tuskegee (USPHS) begun in the 1930s and eventually concluded in the 1970s. In these cases, and others, it might be argued that the pursuit of knowledge took precedence over the well-being and welfare of participants or 'subjects' as they were regarded in such studies.

> **ACTIVITY 1.2**
> Using your online research browser, further investigate the two studies just mentioned, Milgram and the USPHS.
> - How would you feel about participating in these?
> - What aspects would you identify as being unethical?

Activity 1.2 illustrates how issues of deception, suffering, inequality, injustice and even a lack of fundamental principles such as informed consent are evident across these projects. However, our interrogation of these and other similar studies offers us opportunities to develop and advance our ethical thinking and to formulate robust ethical principles. Identifying what you think is unethical about these studies can help you recognize your own ethical principles, which can then shape how you wish to conduct your own research.

One of the most influential approaches to ethical decision-making was developed by Beauchamp and Childress ([1979] 2019). Arising in the biomedical sphere, their approach was designed to support ethical and moral judgements and preserve the rights of research participants. The framework was based on four principles, respect for others (autonomy), acting for the benefit of others (beneficence), doing no harm (nonmaleficence) and equal treatment of all (justice). Such principles were deemed crucial to the fair and equitable treatment of participants and have had considerable consequences for researchers. As you progress through this chapter you might recognize these, or similar underlying principles in other ethical guidelines.

> ### ACTIVITY 1.3
> Research the four principles expressed by Beauchamp and Childress in greater depth
> - Consider whether, and in what ways, these principles were applied to the studies you have just reviewed (Milgram and the USPHS).
> - Apply these principles to the following *dilemma* and consider the possibilities and difficulties you may face.
> - *Dilemma:* A child under the age of 16 years wants to refuse medical treatment. Should this be allowed?

Ethics and ethical thinking are complicated because they are interwoven with the intricacies of human beings and their everyday lives. Ethical debates are never one-sided and ethical answers are seldom straightforward. The history of ethics in human research, or more evidently the lack of ethics in human research, has provided us with useful insights that underpin many of the ethical rules, processes and procedures we follow today. For example, we now should avoid deception, we seek informed consent, we ensure the participants right to withdraw, our research is scrutinized by institutional review committees before we are allowed to step into the research arena and we seek to protect our participants from any harm. Looking back, we can see the benefits that these modifications have brought us, and most particularly, our participants. Looking forward, we might suggest that such transformative thinking has placed limits on researchers and put barriers in the way of certain types of research. Either way, ethics by its very nature invites discussion, and when skilfully debated brings about effective change. However, these recurring debates highlight the continuing subjective and relative nature of what is ethical.

## Ethics: Procedures and Approval

Conventional ideas relating to research ethics regularly take a procedural approach, and students are often introduced to the field from this perspective. All students undertaking primary research with children will need to engage with some form of ethical approval process at the start of their dissertation. Usually, this means the submission of a dissertation proposal to a university ethics committee. For students, the process can engender anxiety and concern and is, of itself, time-limited, whereby failure to receive the longed-for 'approval' is seen as catastrophic. Arguably then, not the most advantageous time to introduce students to the nuances and intricacies of being ethical. The nature of the process tends to focus on extensive bureaucratic hoops, which must be hastily jumped through, and can equally encourage formulaic exploration of procedural ethics and universal principles such as informed consent, confidentiality and anonymity. As Brown, Spiro and Quinto (2020: 750) contend, 'Researchers may perceive ethical applications as little more than a performance, filling out forms in an approved way and using "ethics-speak".' Consequently, students are more likely to encounter ethics as a tick-box exercise, and less likely to engage in discussions about how such procedures do not, of themselves, make us ethical, and furthermore, what might?

As dissertation supervisors and researchers, we have attended and, in many instances, chaired, numerous institutional ethics committees. Despite some inherent challenges within the ethical clearance process, we do not wish to suggest that this practice is unnecessary. On the contrary, we have witnessed the ways in which engagement in this activity can bring important ethical issues out into the open, and equally, how it encourages students to begin, rather than end, their ethical journey. Horgan (2017: 255) states, 'Ethical procedures are crucial to developing ethical literacy in research practitioners and of paramount importance in the research process.' Furthermore, Thomas (2013: 42) proposes that the 'systematic checking' of ethics, by institutional committees, can offer insights into potential risks to participants or others involved in the research, and provide an opportunity to consider and address significant concerns and alternative approaches. The ethics committee then, rather than appearing as an enemy or barrier to your research, instead represents opportunities for you to refine and develop your project, and therefore can be both constructive and supportive.

> **ACTIVITY 1.4**
> In this activity we ask you to examine a range of information related to ethics, from a variety of available sources.
> - Your university's ethical guidelines for research.
> - Broader ethical guidelines, for example, The British Sociological Society and/or The British Psychological Society.
> - Examine the following examples of external links, which relate more specifically to research with children.
> - Ethical Research Involving Children (ERIC). https://childethics.com/ethical-guidance/
> - British Educational Research Association (BERA). https://www.bera.ac.uk/publication/ethical-guidelines-for-educational-research-2018-online
> - NSPCC. https://learning.nspcc.org.uk/research-resources/briefings/research-with-children-ethics-safety-promoting-inclusion

Having explored the various guidelines presented in activity 1.4 it is clear that ethical compliance is crucial to obtaining the positive endorsement of an institutional research ethics committee. As researchers, we are obliged to present an inventory of research conventions, such as confidentiality, with which you are now well-acquainted. The adherence to these protocols can often be constructed as particularly imperative when research involves children.

> **ACTIVITY 1.5**
> This activity helps you to identify fundamental ethical research protocols for your study.
> - Identify as many of these ethical codes of behaviour as you can, for example informed consent and confidentiality.
> - Using evidence from appropriate literature write a paragraph examining each one of these in relation to research with children.

While ethical procedures and issues continually emerge, you may have identified several customary conventions, which are highly pertinent to ethical review bodies and their approval, and even more significant when the research involves children. For example, being called upon to demonstrate how you will gain permission to access participants via schools and/or settings; the requirement of checks from the Disclosure and Barring Service (DBS); the need to obtain informed consent from children, gatekeepers and parents/guardians; the necessity to verify the ability of children to give their own informed consent; the necessary requirement for confidentiality (unless there are safeguarding concerns); insistence on anonymity (even if children are happy for their given name to be used); the rights of children and their families/schools/settings to withdraw from the research at any time; how data will be kept secure; and even or particularly the choice of topic itself. The previous activity, therefore, not only helps you to build the ethical content of your dissertation but also assists you in complying with the required ethical behaviours necessary to carry out your research with children.

The responsibilities of ethics committees are challenging, as they weigh up the perceived risks of your research with the supposed benefits. Equally they must focus on and ensure the upholding of regulations. As researchers we may have experienced, and continue to encounter, what might appear to be frustrating decisions from university ethics committees. Consequently, we may have to amend original proposals and participant-facing documents to comply with conditions imposed by what can seem to be, often faceless and distant committee members. However, we need to recognize that the role of the ethics committee is to enable, rather than impede, your research where possible, protect you and your participants from harm, and safeguard the reputation of the institutions they represent. Therefore, activity 1.6 offers insights into the role of the ethics committee, and the opportunity for you to experience the choices and dilemmas faced by a research ethics committee member.

---

### ACTIVITY 1.6
You are a member of an ethics panel and have been presented with a project proposal where the researcher wants to explore … 'children's everyday perceptions of death'.
- Do you consider this project to be ethical in principle? Why/why not?
- What would you need to know to ensure the research was ethical in practice?

---

## Thinking Ethically about Your Choice of Topic

Activity 1.6 emphasized the weighty responsibilities placed on ethical governance panels, and the key role that topic choice plays in influencing their decisions. What can seem, at the outset, to be a straightforward subject choice, for instance children's perspectives of everyday topics, such as friendships or families, can become a matter for extensive and fervent debate. As Richards, Clark and Boggis (2015: 6) suggest, there is a tendency, when considering research with children, for ethics committees to 'err on the side of caution' and in particular 'to avoid so-called sensitive topics'. This occurs to such an extent, that some topics are considered taboo or off-limits, thus potentially reducing the extent to which children can participate in research.

## ACTIVITY 1.7
This activity asks you to consider the ethical implications of topic choice
- What would you consider to be a sensitive or taboo topic when children are the intended research participants?
- Identify your reasons why?

In answer to the questions posed in activity 1.7 you may have identified subjects such as sex, death or abuse as sensitive subjects. You may have suggested that the reason for this, is because they contain information that we, as adults, prefer not to share with children. Equally, you might articulate the view that we do not want to upset children, rather we aspire to protect them, or when considering younger children, we wish to maintain their innocence. Our own understanding of childhood, and our own life experiences play a significant role in our assigning of judgements about what is, or is not, a sensitive topic. What is construed as a sensitive topic is therefore relative rather than universal. As a student with less research experience, it is unlikely that you would be encouraged to engage with such challenging topics. However, projects that consider children's perspectives of friendships, families and healthy eating, do not, at first glance, appear to be quite so controversial. However, our experience with ethics committees informs us that this is not the case, and therefore what determines a sensitive topic, and the reasons they are deemed to be so, is not always immediately obvious. Consequently, all topic choices require, and are given, substantial levels of scrutiny, resulting from adult concerns regarding the capacity of children to understand the substantive elements of research, and their ability to provide authentic informed consent for it.

At this point, you might be wondering what could be ethically problematic about discussing friendship with children. However, consider the child who lacks friends or is being bullied. How might their well-being be affected by talking about friendships? How might we overcome this to allow researchers to explore friendship without making participants feel uncomfortable? We could, for example, change the question from 'can you tell us about your friendships' to 'what makes a good friend'. The first approach questions children's personal experiences of friendships, which could be negative, whilst the other explores the concept of friendship in more abstract, and therefore less personal, terms. Both questions will get the researcher the necessary data relating to children's perceptions of friendship, but one is perhaps less ethically sensitive than the other. Equally, you might wonder about the problematic nature of discussing healthy eating. Consider putting the child in a situation where the meals provided by their families are found wanting against current policies of what is considered healthy eating for children. Furthermore, in challenging economic climates, families might struggle to provide healthy options. Under such circumstances the child may be made to feel that their family is different or in some way inadequate. Rather than ask what a child eats you could ask them to creatively construct a plate of food and tell you about the food choices they have made. Here we can see ways in which the same topic can be ethically explored through adapting the approach taken and the questions asked.

---

### ACTIVITY 1.8

Having read the previous examples, which illustrate how research topics might be modified to comply with ethical sensitivities, consider how you might adapt or develop the following topic exploring children's perceptions of family.
- What do you think would be an inappropriate question to ask children about their family. For example, 'are your Mum and Dad married'?
- What is inappropriate about this?
- How might you approach the topic of family with children in a more ethical way?

---

Hydén (2008) suggests that almost any topic can be identified as sensitive, while Martins, Oliveira and Tendais (2018) highlight topic sensitivity as variable among individuals but propose strong links to age, developmental stage and life experience. Thereby, raising an ethical alarm for research with children. Consequently, the combination of immaturity and subject-matter seemingly presents ethics committees with a double jeopardy. Tensions appear between time-honoured constructions of a vulnerable, innocent and developmentally immature child, with the portrayal of the agentic and competent child, often constructed throughout a research proposal. Despite, the researcher's inclusion of thoughtful and critical ontological, methodological and ethical arguments, promoting the centrality of the care and well-being of participants, the at-risk child is more readily constructed by the panel, which then prioritizes protectionism and questions the validity of the proposal. As Powell and colleagues (2019: 326) argue, despite a 'growing consensus around the value of engaging children in social research, researchers often report that the recruitment of children can be challenging, with tensions around children's participation amplified when the research involves sensitive topics'. As topic choice, overtly sensitive or not, has a propensity to destabilize the equilibrium of ethics panel members, it is clear that solid evidence of ethical procedure, appropriate choice of methods and fitting philosophical underpinnings are required to reduce disquiet and promote assurances of moral compliance.

As noted above, a clear-cut way to navigate the ethical process is to ensure that your research methodology, methods and ethics are fully aligned and explained. For example, qualitative methodologies, discussed further in the next chapter, are not only deemed highly suitable for research with children but also for those topics considered to be sensitive. The reason for this is the adoption of an interpretive, naturalistic approach that aims to empower the child to participate and have their voice heard. The selected issue is thus explored from the child's own perspective, and the meanings they bring to it. The subsequent ethical discussions, can then focus on the participants [and researcher/s], emphasizing care, emotional support and well-being, and advancing the merits of ongoing reflexive conversations. The ethical details discussed above need to be made evident in your application for ethical approval, and the next section outlines these requirements.

## Assembling Your Ethics Application

Successful ethics applications need to provide a comprehensive and clear framework of your research, how you wish to carry it out and with whom. This involves not only a research proposal and completion of an ethics form but also a range of associated paperwork. The compilation of these various documents can be challenging but each helps to provide consistent knowledge of your endeavour. Each document also addresses questions that an ethics committee requires to make an informed decision regarding the progression of your study. This paperwork is also necessary for your recruitment activities once approval has been granted. Starting with activity 1.9, this section provides details of the necessary documentation and their content, to help you identify and assemble what is required.

> **ACTIVITY 1.9**
> What information would you consider necessary for an ethics committee to approve your ethics application?
> - Draw up a list and then check with ours below.

Your research proposal and all the documents accompanying it need to be totally consistent. For example, your research title and your research aim/s and objectives need to be the same across all forms of documentation. The method you will use should also be identical, so the ethics committee know exactly what you intend to do. Any discrepancies across the documentation will ensure that ethics panel members cannot fully understand what you are trying to do and therefore cannot give their approval. A strong relationship between your method, methodology and ethics must be evident and well defined to produce a coherent narrative for ethics panel members to engage with. If your methodology promotes children's voices your methods need to ensure that children can speak, and your ethics should hold the principles of rights and voice. Our list below is intended to be indicative of what is required, rather than exhaustive, and additional information may be necessary depending on your topic, participants and/or approach.

1. **Evidence of Disclosure and Barring Service (DBS) check:** If you intend to carry out research in a setting, such as a school or nursery, the ethics panel will need evidence of an up-to-date DBS clearance.

2. **Research proposal:** This is your chance to present your proposed research to your supervisor and the university ethics committee. Although the word count of this document is usually relatively short, the thought that goes into it is considerable, so do not underestimate the time it will take. In discussions with your supervisor your initial ideas may change, they may solidify and/or alter, but this is all part of the process and with it comes greater clarity. Your proposal must be written clearly and concisely. Try to avoid any vagaries, ambiguities, uncertainties or inconsistencies. The key features of your methodology, methods and ethics should relate clearly to each other. For example, avoid a methodology that speaks of the importance of child voice if your method is observation. The contents of a research proposal often include features such as a working title; an introduction or background to your research; concise aims and objectives; a brief literature review; a clear methodology with fitting plans for access and recruitment of participants, appropriate research methods and ethical considerations; a research schedule as well as all information and consent documentation.

3. **Recruitment strategy:** Here you will explain your plans to access recruits. You can indicate approximately how many participants you need, and if there are any specific age requirements. If you have access to a setting it is inclusive to invite the whole class to participate in your activity. From our experience gaining consent from all the children in the class is highly unlikely but have a plan about how you

might conduct you research with all who choose to consent. You will also need to provide information to any relevant gatekeepers, such as head teachers and classroom teachers who will need to consent to your research and provide access.

4. **Research schedule:** Here you provide a realistic plan of your research timetable, highlighting significant landmarks throughout the research within given timeframes. The schedule demonstrates your organizational abilities, and acts as a guide to your progress. Key phases to emphasize might include, the start and end dates of data collection, a timeframe for analysing your data, a schedule for writing particular sections of your dissertation, and finally time to read, reflect on and edit your work towards the end of the project.

5. **Information letters and consent:** Information letters are extremely important. They must contain all the information required for the receiver to make an informed choice about their participation. They must be clear, concise and as these documents not only represent yourself but also the university, they must be faultless containing no spelling mistakes or typographical errors. You will need to provide appropriate information to a range of participants in your research; children, parents/guardians and gatekeepers.

    a. **Information/consent for children:** Will require an age-appropriate explanation of their anticipated involvement. Information letters and consent forms for young children can be less formal but still include explanations of key terms. It might be useful to explain what research means, how long the child will be involved in the research and what they will have to do. Equally, it is important to explain the children's right to withdraw, to confidentiality and how their data will be used. When constructing these letters think of them in terms of them being colourful, accessible and creatively designed, rather than text-heavy narratives.

b **Information/consent for gatekeepers:** You will also need to seek permission and provide information to the gatekeepers of your chosen setting that might be the headteacher or the nursery setting manager. Parents/guardians also need appropriate information to make an informed choice regarding their child's participation. If your research is exploring what might be construed as a sensitive topic you will also need to demonstrate awareness of participant well-being and highlight organizations of support relating to topic.

Therefore, all your documentation should demonstrate your knowledge of ethics and illustrate how you will behave in the field when making ethical decisions. Your research proposal therefore should exemplify your ethical capacity. How will you do this? Whilst completing activity 1.10 think about how you might include such content in your research proposal.

---

### ACTIVITY 1.10
You are conducting research about friendships in childhood.
- How would you support or respond to a child who becomes upset during your data collection?
- What would you do in the moment and what would you do later?

---

The ethics panel wish to see evidence of how you will respond under such circumstances. The information provided can reassure ethics committee members that you will behave using sound ethical principles in your practice. The ethics committee are looking for an application that is clear, coherent, and consistent and demonstrates your knowledge and understanding of the ethics involved. Part of this consistency can be enhanced by recognizing the relationships between method and methodology. This is something that students might initially find challenging. However, it is important to recognize the synergy between what you are looking for, how you attempt to find it and the links between your research aims, methodology, method and ultimately ethics.

> **ACTIVITY 1.11**
> Identify the inconsistencies evident below and what might be problematic in relation to ethics in the following proposal
> - Aim: To explore children's perceptions of playing in the sandbox.
> - Methodology: Promoting children's rights, agency and voice.
> - Method: Observation.

However, approval from an ethics committee and the application content itself do not of themselves make you ethical. So having explored what an ethical application looks like we now move on to examine the practice of behaving ethically in the field.

## Ethics: Principles and Practice

The previous section illustrates the importance of ethical procedures in the research process. Notwithstanding such arguments, following these ethical rules and regulations without critical consideration raises questions, to which there are seldom any straightforward answers. Grbich (2004) argues that traditional grand narratives in relation to the research process focus on the dedicated following of rules in relation to canonical aspects of research, such as informed consent, confidentiality, right to withdraw and so on. Furthermore, this blind adherence to directives which promote universal ethical and moral systems should be regarded with scepticism, emphasizing instead 'individually responsible research and respect for others' (Grbich 2004: 90). Similarly, Shiraani, Shaheer and Carr (2022: 21) suggest that 'there is a need to move beyond procedural ethics to capture ethics in practice and to critically recognize what it takes to be ethical when undertaking research'. Equally, the online platform Ethical Research Involving Children (ERIC 2019) assumes that 'ethics is much more than procedural compliance with a prescribed set of rules or code of conduct that can deliver good or safe research in any given context. While such codes play an important role, the ERIC approach recognises the many ways in which researchers' own knowledge, beliefs, assumptions, values, attitudes, and experience intersect with ethical decision-making.'

We concur, evidenced by our own research encounters, that it is our multiple everyday selves and the moral principles we maintain that support and guide our ethical practice. Plummer (2001) highlights how we draw on our everyday experiences, choices and decisions during our research. Similarly, that being an ethical/moral researcher involves a commitment to 'the value of the human being', 'an ethic of care and compassion', 'a politics of recognition and respect' and 'the importance of trust' (Plummer 2008: 482–3). Furthermore, Plummer (2001: 228) identifies what he calls 'the five great ethical principles of current times', each one being there to guide researchers through the complexities of the moral maze; recognition and tolerance; caring for others; equality, fairness and justice; autonomy, freedom and choice; and minimizing harm. For us this is where ethics becomes part of what we do and who we are and is therefore so much more than procedural hoops. Our ethical principles inform and shape our every decision and their outcomes, and we often reflect on these decisions long afterwards. Principles relating to children's rights, safety, well-being and inclusion, the importance of respect, relationships and trust, and the need for reflexivity to inform our critical practice are central to how we conduct research and are integral aspects of our ethical practice.

During a previous activity you were asked to explore the procedural aspects of ethical guidelines. You may also have noted underlying principles that support the ways in which these organizations work with children. Activity 1.12 asks you to extend and broaden these principles for a better understanding of such, often neglected, philosophies, which can strengthen research with children.

> **ACTIVITY 1.12**
> With Plummer's arguments in mind what would you consider to be the key principles in research with children?
> - How might you apply these to your own research?

You may have identified the straightforward aspects of voice, agency and participation as some of these key principles. These are also central features of methodologies for doing research with children (see the next chapter). Enabling children to have a voice, be agentic and participate become ethical pursuits and shape our actions in research. Being ethical is far more involved than providing the right to withdraw and gaining consent, it involves how we enable children to feel empowered, active and involved. Such ethical principles call on us to promote our participants' well-being and welfare in each and every interaction. This then is the emotional work of articulating ethical principles into ethical practice and can be referred to as an 'ethic of care' (see Coombs and Richards 2023). For us, an ethic of care is a key principle that we embrace in all our research practice, and so can be found in our research proposals, discussions and practices.

This ethic of care, emerged from feminist standpoints, and emphasizes the importance of relevant ethical principles and the importance of combining these into research practice. For instance, the value of mutually beneficial participant–researcher relationships, the care and well-being of participants, investment in respect, reciprocity and empowerment. Wall (2010: 3) contends that feminism has 'effectively challenged ethicists and others to reimagine human life in terms such as care, relationality, embodiment and power'. This ethical principle continues to shape our interactions with children in our research projects. It informs the language we use, the activities we select and privileges the supremacy of their welfare above our research goals. Consider therefore whether an ethic of care is an appropriate inclusion in your own methodology and ethics.

# [Un]Ethical Vignettes

In many research projects, situations arise in which researchers are required to make unanticipated ethical decisions, and where our principles must inform our practice. Below you will encounter some of these ethical moments that arose across several of our own, and our students', research projects. These situations were not foreseen or prepared for, and therefore impromptu or so-called ad hoc ethical decisions were made in-the-moment. As you read through the vignettes below, contemplate what it is that makes these situations a cause for ethical reflection, also try and put yourself in the position of the researcher and think about how you might respond to such circumstances.

## Vignette 1: Grandad's Ashes

A small focus group was held to discuss everyday aspects of death with young people aged fourteen years. In an attempt to open up the conversation, the participants were asked to bring ordinary objects from home that evoked death for them. One participant brought along his grandfather's ashes in a container, which provoked some excited discussions. Unprompted, he removed the lid from the container and invited his fellow participants to look inside. Enthusiastic reactions followed, resulting in an invitation from the participant, for the other members of the group to put their hands into the container and touch the ashes.

At this point, I (Sarah Coombs), feeling rather anxious that grandad's ashes might end up on the floor and require sweeping up, asked the group to consider their feelings about the proposed move. The result being that the participants decided not to go ahead and, much to my relief, the container was closed.

- From a perspective of an ethic of care why might the researcher be anxious?

- What do you consider to be the ethical issues positioned in this encounter?

- Which relationships in this research encounter require careful consideration and sensitivity on the part of the researcher?

- What might be the emotional repercussions for the participant who brought the ashes in, the other participants involved, and the parents and guardians. Why is the emotional well-being of these individuals' part of the ethical responsibility of the researcher?

- What would you have done as the researcher?

## Vignette 2: Too 'Naughty' to Take Part

A research colleague and I arrived at a school to conduct a piece of research into young people's perspectives of well-being. On arrival we were informed that one of the participants, who had provided both his own and his parents' consent, would not be taking part. We enquired 'why', assuming the young person must be unwell. The school's response was that on the previous day, the young person's behaviour had been particularly difficult, and therefore the school had decided that he could no longer take part. This was his 'punishment'.

- Consider the various power relationships within this scenario.

- How might the ethical procedures and principles put in place by the researchers be compromised by the gatekeeper's decision?

- What options did the researchers have? What would you have done?

## Vignette 3: Taking Part: A Student Research Project

This research project was to take place in the school in which the student already had an existing relationship. The student had secured permission and informed consent from the school, the class teacher, the children and their parents. The research, a drawing activity with recorded conversations on the chosen research topic took place in a small, partitioned area of the classroom. Notwithstanding the prior consent, on the actual day of the research, the student took the opportunity to ensure that all the children remained happy to take part and understood they could stop at any point (ongoing verbal consent). One child, after drawing a picture, decided they would like to leave, and in the spirit of on-going consent the child safely returned to their original class. Some moments later however, the teacher brought the child back to the research table telling the child 'you're supposed to be here', and the child stayed. Finding herself in this situation the student was unsure what to do. She came to the next supervision very distressed, believing her actions to be unethical as she felt she had not protected the child's right to withdraw.

- There is an assumption that researchers are powerful but how empowered was the student researcher in this situation?
- In settings where gatekeepers have alternative ideas of children's agency, how effective can ethical principles like the right to withdraw be?
- What are the implications for informed consent here?

## Vignette 4: 'Selecting' Participants

This incident occurred in the context of a local primary school. The student researcher had worked there for some time and had a good relationship with the school team. The student sent information letters and consent forms to all the children, the school and the parents/guardians of the class she worked in, as indicative of an inclusive and child-focused methodology. As the student was not in the setting every day, the headteacher offered to help by having the consent forms returned directly to him. The student agreed that this would be a good idea. On their return to work, the student went to collect the forms and the headteacher helpfully reported that the forms had been filtered, and the six 'best' participants for project, chosen and informed.

- Using some of the discussions in the previous vignettes consider what ethical issues are presented here?
- As the researcher, how empowered would you feel to contest the headteacher's actions?
- How would you respond?

Having looked at these scenarios, a common theme that you might have identified is the significance of power relations in research. Your ideas about agency, voice, and participation and how they shape the ethical structure of your research may be incompatible with the ideas and context in which they occur. This ethical dance is something researchers will encounter when working with children, requiring diplomacy, whilst also attempting to remain true to your principles. There are no easy answers to these ethical dilemmas, but your decisions reveal you as an ethical researcher.

Exploring the above vignettes brings ethics out of procedural protocols and into everyday research situations. For a number of reasons, such instances are often not written about or reflected upon (Richards and Coombs 2023). First, they may make the researcher feel uncomfortable. Second, the researcher may fear they are being judged as unethical by their peers. Third, exploration of such issues can be regarded as rather self-indulgent. However, when such things happen in research, we contend it is helpful to reflexively consider them rather than hide them away. It is how we respond to these situations that reveal who we are as ethical researchers, and it is how, when we reflect upon them that we are thinking ethically. Both Foucault (1972) and Zignon (2008) argue that it is only when we confront ethical dilemmas and reflect on the principles and practices that inform our research that we are actually thinking ethically.

## Ethics: Beyond the Participant

Many students rationalize that choosing a research study without the involvement of human participants will be an ethics-free or ethics-light option, and their research proposals regularly reflect this. Bold statements are made, whereby the lack of human participants is said to negate the need for ethical consideration. To an extent this viewpoint has some, if limited, merit. Certainly, the canonical procedural ethics, discussed earlier, lack specific relevance. However, the absence of actual participants calls you to draw on the research of others for your data, and so you may find yourself entangled in their ethical debates and discussions. Similarly, you must consider the ethics involved in presenting the work of others in an honest, reliable and trustworthy way. No researcher wants to see their work misrepresented, changed or misused. Likewise, you should consider your own ethical position within the research. You should engage reflexively with your chosen topic, pinpoint the reasons why you elected to investigate this area. Highlight your own subjectivity within the project. This does not mean a passionate polemic on researcher bias is necessary, rather an acknowledgement of self/selves within your research, and this recognition made into an explicit strength from which reflexive practice emerges. Reflexivity is therefore a central ethical feature within this type of research, as your motivations, positions, values and emotions become central to the project and your ethical deliberations.

> **ACTIVITY 1.13**
> Produce a paragraph that explores the ethics involved in a dissertation that does not involve human participants.
> - Consider concepts such as subjectivity, positionality and reflexivity (for support see Chapter 4).

# Over to You

Part of the purpose of a dissertation is, for you as a student, to learn about and engage with ethical procedures, principles and practices. Writing about the ethical situations that occurred in your research can effectively demonstrate the learning that has taken place. Do not, therefore, restrict the ethical content of your dissertation to simply highlighting the procedural aspects of ethics but instead write about the dilemmas you have faced. For examples of how researchers reflexively write about this (see Richards and Coombs 2023).

Our aspiration is that your consideration of ethics is now no longer confined to the traditional bureaucratic silo to which it has so often been assigned, but rather you can see how ethics can run through the entirety of your work. An ethical discourse or story can be the foundation of your research project. As Hesse-Biber and Levy (2011: 77) contend, 'ethics exist within a social context', and within this context we have obligations, some of which do not of themselves make us ethical. To explore this claim further, consider the social contexts in the above vignettes. In each of these examples we see the limitations of bureaucratic ethical procedures in helping researchers respond to particular circumstances. It is not therefore the information and consent documentation or the approval of an ethics committee that ensure ethical practice it is you as the researcher acting in the moment, making your decisions. Reinharz (1997: 3) describes the self as 'the key fieldwork tool' and it is this, and the many selves we bring and situate throughout our research that provide us with opportunities for ethical growth and reflexivity.

To take the next steps, try activity 1.14 and the ethical content of your proposal should begin to take shape. Consider structuring your ethics content in a similar way to the presentation of this chapter, beginning with ethical procedures, and following with ethical principles and practices.

---

**ACTIVITY 1.14**

Choose a topic that you would like to explore with children.
- Examine how the procedures and principles outlined in this chapter can be applied to your proposal in order to build an ethical discourse throughout.

---

# Conclusion

We hope this chapter has made the complex topic of ethics, in relation to your overall research project, seem more accessible and less daunting. Possibly, ethics can now be considered as an everyday notion rather than a remote and erudite concept. At the outset of the chapter, we emphasized the ways in which ethics is frequently conceptualized as either a hoop to be jumped through or something to be afraid of. Moreover, once the ethical boxes are ticked and our fears discarded, we need not be troubled by such issues again. However, notwithstanding such views, we can now position ethics as useful, valuable even, providing clarity to ethical procedures, expression to ethical principles, morality to ethical practice and centrality to our ethical endeavours.

The chapter highlights the ethical procedures we are invited to follow in order to submit a research proposal to an institutional ethics panel. These well-trodden ethical processes arguably deliver constraints but also offer reassurances and new possibilities. Furthermore, we have observed and established the importance of a variety of ethical principles and values, which underpin our research with children and largely emanate from ourselves. Such principles form a firm foundation, promoting children's rights, voice, care and well-being, which transform into, and become, our ethical practice. We note here the complexities of balancing these three central tenets whilst also engaging in critical debates, culminating in our emergence as critical-ethical and moral researchers.

Through the vignettes provided, we see how the best laid plans of researchers can go awry, and equally how the decisions we make in those moments shape our ethical practice. The unplanned and often-ambiguous nature of such incidents means there are seldom straightforward or simple answers to such dilemmas. However, the combination of how we respond and how we reflect in the aftermath contributes to our ethical growth as reflexive practitioners. Reflexive analysis of this type, not only when mishaps occur, but when considering your dissertation in its entirety is an insightful and valid inclusion, making yourself visible and promoting your ethical self and moral integrity to the forefront of your discussions. Researchers should and must follow standard ethical procedures but are equally obliged to behave ethically.

# 2

# Navigating the Methodological Maze

## Introduction

The intention of this chapter is to demystify the term and role of methodology and help you develop a methodology for your own dissertation. The very word *methodology* is often viewed with trepidation. When questioned by dissertation supervisors, students often respond nervously with, 'I never did quite understand it'. Methodology can be perceived as an obscure and incomprehensible concept, a notion shrouded in confusion, and therefore one that might usefully be ignored, and/or briefly glossed over, for fear of getting it wrong. Consequently, students sometimes happily opt for the more solid ground of *methods* as a recognizable and tempting discussion, distant from the assumed vagaries of the methodological maze. However, an omission of methodological thinking in research projects is glaring, and getting to grips with it is important, and dare we say, enjoyable. Therefore, the ambition of this chapter is to position methodology as a collection of accessible and user-friendly ideas (approaches, theories, philosophies, ways of seeing), which when combined with a childhood studies research project help to form a solid and critical base from which to build your dissertation.

The different perspectives that can be brought together to form a methodology can be likened to the ingredients for baking a cake or the foundations for building a house. Such approaches, individually or when combined, can help facilitate direction and clarity through, what might otherwise, appear to be a muddle of perplexing ideas. The components of the methodology are way more exciting and far less constraining than you might think, allowing us to broaden our horizons in expansive, original and even more critical ways. Well-established theories, concepts and ideas are, without a doubt, the basic constituents of any methodology. However, the choice of these is profoundly informed by your own values, beliefs and ethical/moral understandings of what research with children is and should be. Such ingredients once identified and blended become a constant set of principles and practices that guide you through the twists and turns of your research project.

Your choice of methodology, and it is *your* choice, delivers a foundation that underpins your work from the title to the aims of your study, the methods used, the analysis of data and the writing up. In short, the methodology is an integral and significant part of your dissertation, which not only forms and informs your research but brings together many seemingly disparate parts. It therefore requires thoughtful and extensive consideration. However, in order to develop a methodological position, it is common for students to maximize their library quota and explore every book they can find relating to research methods, in the hope of discovering the perfect methodological match for their study. To briefly return to our baking analogy, this is akin to finding an off-the-shelf packet-mix containing the perfect components for your cake, unfortunately, as with many quick-fixes the results are often formulaic rather than individual to your study. However, you might search more productively in a place you least expect to find the answer, that is, within yourself. This somewhat-ambiguous statement will make more sense as you progress through this chapter. We promise.

The discussions here should not be viewed as a comprehensive guide from which to choose assorted and available methodologies, although some examples will be given. Rather, it should be regarded as a companion, which aims to support you in producing a research project with a solid and coherent methodological structure and the consequent and consistent threads that can run throughout your work. Therefore, rather than fearing the seemingly impenetrable and perplexing uncertainties of the methodological maze, we hope this chapter will help you discover the thrill of creating your own appropriate methodological approach. The chapter asks key questions for your consideration and response. For example, what is a methodology, how do we begin to construct one, and what are the connections between methodological approaches and other aspects of your dissertation. Most importantly, the chapter examines why your own ideas and values are central to developing your methodology, and therefore the methodological relationship between yourself, your research choices and your project.

## What Is a Methodology?

To begin our explorations of what a methodology is we wish to return to our analogy of baking a cake. Consider what would you need to do before you start? First, decide what type of cake you want to make, read a few recipes, collect ingredients, gather utensils, turn on the oven, line the cake tin and so on. Alternatively, you could, as previously suggested, opt for that packet of cake mix, where everything is pre-measured allowing you to just mix and go. This second option sounds enticing and, when considering methodology, attractive for its off-the-shelf, instant results. However, choosing a methodology in this way although quickly gratifying may not fit well with your specific project. Basically, it is someone else's vision. A delicious cake calls for your own subjective ideas about flavour, texture and visual appearance. In a similar way your methodology will be emblematic of your values and ideas, a clear notion of what you want to achieve, a plan for reaching your goal and a critical understanding of why you are taking this approach.

> ### ACTIVITY 2.1
> With the cake as a methodological analogy, consider the following questions.
> - What is your favourite cake and why?
> - What ingredients are needed?
> - In what way is each of the ingredients important for the end result?
> - What relationship/s do you have with this cake?
> - How does it make you feel?
> - Does it matter if someone makes it in a different way?

Completing activity 2.1 should have helped you recognize that building your methodology is about selecting key concepts and/or philosophical ideas to create a recipe that is unique to you. Defining just what a methodology is, however, can be challenging.

Activity 2.2 is provided here to help you begin to explore, formulate and refine your thoughts around methodology by reviewing relevant sources of literature.

> ### ACTIVITY 2.2
> You will find sections dedicated to defining methodology in a wide range of social science research textbooks. In academic journals you will find examples where the researcher's methodological approach is discussed. Utilizing both sources can help you to begin to formulate your methodological ideas. Therefore, select a range of literature sources for definitions of methodology and journal articles related to your potential research approach.
> - First, reflect on definitions of methodology and then write them in your own words.
> - Second, read research papers where researchers have presented their methodologies, and then list the key concepts they use, for example interpretivism.

Your choice of sources has perhaps begun to solidify your understanding of the term 'methodology' and its application. Reviewing your list from activity 2.2 helps you to conceptualize methodology as a group or collection of different philosophical and theoretical ideas from which to build your methodology. For some students it is the word itself that can initially pose a problem, as it appears to prioritize and implicate the methods we use to gather our research data. For example, interviews, surveys, focus groups and so on better resemble the utensils used to make a cake rather than the key ingredients. The methodology, however, is not just our method[s], although, as we shall see, they are inextricably linked. To clarify the difference but connection between methodology and methods, Bhatt (2012: 160) contends that methodology 'guides' our dissertation and methods are practical 'techniques' we use to collect data. Equally, Hesse-Biber and Leavey (2011: 7) define methodology as, 'the bridge that brings our philosophical standpoint ... and method ... together'. Therefore, if we combine these two viewpoints, our methodology becomes imbued with both guiding and underpinning values and principles that link directly to our practices and methods. Understandably, the fundamental beliefs we choose within our methodologies are highly likely to align to our own attitudes and assumptions about how we see the world and the children in it. In these choices, you, as an individual, are reflected in your methodology.

As researchers we often have clear ideas about our topic, the aims of our research and the methods we want to use but are less sure and able to articulate the philosophies and values on which they stand. This is when your own choices start to emerge and determine your methodology, as you begin to ask yourself a number of questions; what topic do I want to explore; what questions do I want to ask; how do I want to uncover the answers; and how do I view the world and the children in it.

# Perspectives on Childhood and Links to Methodology

Chapters throughout this volume illustrate the long tradition of involving children in research. However, historically this child and consequently all children were seen as one homogeneous group, objectified and almost exclusively scrutinized from the perspective of adults. Similarly, children were conceptualized as vulnerable, incompetent, passive, unreliable, not to be taken too seriously and having little to say of any value. Viewed from this position, children had only a limited contribution to make to the all-powerful adult world, and thus childhoods were marginalized, silenced and 'othered', until such time as children reached the culmination of their journey, that is becoming an adult. Research underpinned by such values was and remains a potential ideological and methodological position, leading to particular approaches to childhood research.

---

**ACTIVITY 2.3**
Consider this viewpoint that children are vulnerable, passive and have little to say.
- Which methodological values can you identify that would exemplify or reproduce these assumptions about children?
- From this perspective how important might children's views be in a research project?
- What would the involvement of children in such research look like?

---

As students of childhood, and potential researchers in this field, your opinions of children and childhoods may differ from the constructions present in activity 2.3 and alternative perspectives form the underlying principles of your own methodological position. For example, you might be influenced by work emanating from the 1980s/1990s, the so-called 'new' social studies of childhood. This then emerging paradigm, led by the theorizing of James and Prout (1997), called for a move away from entrenched, and arguably outmoded, ideas about children and rather encouraged alternative ways of conceptualizing childhoods. The central tenets of this approach acknowledged the varied and complex lives of children and the acceptance of a multiplicity of different childhoods, rather than one homogeneous group. Children became positioned as active and competent social agents with rights to participate in research and have their voices heard. Children's voices became an expert and legitimate source of knowledge, and at last, it seemed that children were becoming worthy of study in and on their own terms.

> **ACTIVITY 2.4**
> Consider the viewpoint that children are active social agents, with rights to participate in research and have their voices heard.
> - Which methodological values can you identify that would exemplify or reproduce these assumptions about children?
> - From this perspective how important might children's views be in a research project?
> - What would the involvement of children in such research look like?

The implications of this reconceptualization, with its values centred on children's agency, voice, rights and participation, led to a rapid expansion in research *with*, rather than *on*, children. Researchers argued for more child-centred and participatory research methods, endeavouring to uncover the lived experiences of children through their own words.

> **ACTIVITY 2.5**
> The changing constructions of children and childhoods also led to alternative research methods that focused on research *with* children and children's participation.
> - From this perspective identify some of the methods that would be considered appropriate for this approach, and therefore fit with the values embedded in this methodological approach.

Potentially, your responses to activity 2.5 will be wide-ranging, identifying both methods and activities in which children can confidently participate, including arts-based projects, focus group conversations, guided tours for adult researchers of the contexts in which children live and many others. All these, seek direct insights into children's social worlds and aim to reveal first-hand experiences of children's daily lives. The connection between methodological approach and research method should therefore be coming more clear. However, change is continuous and as Canosa and Graham (2020: 29) suggest, as research with children evolves and changes, critical tensions arise, which look to challenge central theories, meanings, and tenets such as 'voice', 'agency' and 'participation'. Whilst such arguments may seem daunting to engage with, daring to unpick some of these in greater depth, should provide a more nuanced and critical analysis of your research project and help to define and re-define your discussions.

As students of childhood, you will be aware of two well-established and dominant views of children and childhood, both of which we can draw on to help us find our way through the methodological maze, they are perhaps not always as mutually exclusive as they initially may seem. For example, Lahman (2008) contends that children can be both competent and vulnerable simultaneously. Children can indeed be both, and such complexities can inform our thinking, our attitudes and beliefs and ultimately our methodological approach. What is emerging here is our acknowledgement that our first steps to forming our methodological position are to scrutinize our own influences and ideas about what children and childhood are.

## How to Begin to Construct Your Own Methodology?

With the alternative perspectives on children and childhoods, and emerging thoughts about the presence of self in methodology uppermost in our minds, we move on to identify the components required to build your own methodology.

We start with activity 2.6, which should help you to acknowledge your own values about children in research.

> **ACTIVITY 2.6**
> Begin my exploring your own views on children and childhoods.
> - Define your view of a child.
> - With this view in mind, what involvement do you think children should have in research and why?
> - Identify how these views influence the ways in which you might carry out research with children.

The way you responded to activity 2.6 points to the potential underlying principles and approaches of your research methodology. In short, this is your ontological position, that is your stance on children and childhood, which then influences your epistemological position, that is the type of knowledge you seek and how you will attempt to find it. Therefore, when you start to scrutinize your responses to the questions posed in activity 2.6 you can begin to see your own perspective on children and childhoods emerging as relevant to, and embedded in, your methodology. Your framework may fit neatly with ideas of children as either competent or incompetent, childhood as a biological fact or a social construction, the child as agentic or vulnerable, or potentially both. How you view children will therefore be revealed in the ways you wish to include or exclude them in your research, and these values shape the choice of your research ingredients, or methodology.

> **ACTIVITY 2.7**
> After activity 2.6 you could potentially find yourself leaning towards the methodological ingredients that focus on children's rights and participation in research. You should explore these ideas further here.
> - What rights do you think children should have and how might you facilitate these in your research generally but in your methodology specifically?

In responding to the activities presented thus far in this chapter you are now beginning to think methodologically. We imagine that it is becoming clear to you that the choices you face methodologically are significantly influenced by your own values and beliefs. Therefore, who you are in everyday life motivates and inspires the ways in which you feel research with children should be carried out, and how you will do that in the field. Perhaps now is a good time to begin writing about your ideas and forming the foundations of your dissertation methodology. Activity 2.8 will help you start this process.

> **ACTIVITY 2.8**
> List the ideas that you feel underlie qualitative methodological approaches to research with children. It is these that underpin and strengthen your own methodology.
> - Find definitions of the following: children's agency, voice, rights and participation.
> - Put these into your own words by writing a short paragraph on each from a research perspective.
> - Think of methods that enable you to use such ideas and consider how you could apply them into your research.

## Some Useful Methodological Features in Research with Children

So far, the ideas we have encouraged you to consider and apply to your methodology relate to assumptions around the social construction of childhood. Following on from this we now outline some of the normative values related to qualitative research more generally, which should also be integral to your methodology.

One possible philosophical standpoint that you are highly likely to have explored during your research methods modules is positivism. This approach is based on the values of objectivity, generalizability, measurability and repeatability. Such principles are embedded in positivist methodologies and therefore clearly inform the methods chosen. If you think back over your studies, you might be able to identify some of the central tenets of this approach. Experimental methods may come to mind, those that develop and test a hypothesis, manipulate variables and analyse numerical data from often quantitative surveys or questionnaires. All of these would be appropriate in supporting a positivist methodology. Thomas (2013: 108) identifies that the philosophical foundation of such an approach is 'realism', searching for an objective truth that leaves little room for interpretation. In research with children this approach is not always conducive to, or easily reconciled with, our previous discussions around children's agency and participation in the research process, which reveals subjective and multiple rather than singular truths. Here then truth becomes a relative concept. Methodologically the presence of many truths in research is available through the lens of interpretivism. The values inherent within this concept obviously diverge from those of positivism and through relativism are integral to qualitative research.

## Methodological Feature: Interpretivism

---

### ACTIVITY 2.9
Read around the topic of interpretivism.
- Identify definitions of interpretivism and its central tenets.
- Write a paragraph that puts these ideas into your own words.
- Consider the implications of this approach for your own methodology.

---

In response to activity 2.9 perhaps you will have uncovered some of the following ideas related to the interpretivist paradigm. The focus of interpretivism is on human participants, their views, meanings and understandings of the social world in which they live. In opposition to the philosophical foundations of realism found within positivism, interpretivism is based on *relativism*, and thus emphasizes the social construction of reality by individuals, and the prominence of the contexts in which they exist. From this perspective our comprehension of a subject area develops through the insights offered by our participants. Hesse-Biber and Leavey (2011: 17) identify that these approaches focus on 'understanding, interpretation and social meaning', thereby looking at the subjective experience of individuals, the sharing of ideas and conversations, and the co-construction of meaning through interaction. The purpose of having interpretivism within a methodological framework is to acknowledge that there are multiple ways of seeing the world, all of which are representative of multiple truths and realities. Equally, there are many ways to interpret data, each of which can be authentic, legitimate and valid.

## Methodological Feature: Qualitative Research

The central tenets of interpretivism sit well with qualitative research, which although belonging to many disciplines, works particularly well in research with children.

---

### ACTIVITY 2.10
Read around the topic of qualitative research.
- Identify definitions of qualitative research and its central tenets.
- Write a paragraph that puts these ideas into your own words.
- Consider the implications of this approach for your own methodology.

---

Qualitative research tends to be exploratory in nature, and your research project may aim to do just that, explore children's perspectives of a particular topic. As experienced dissertation supervisors we have seen many such studies, which have thoughtfully and creatively highlighted children's perceptions of their everyday lives. For example, children's views on healthy eating, climate change, family, friendships, beauty and many more. Students sometimes worry that qualitative approaches will generate insufficient data. However, once immersed in the analysis of their time spent with the children, possibly talking, drawing pictures, creating a collage or taking photographs, they find the ensuing data to be rich, complex and unique. The outcomes of such qualitative, participatory methodology can bring children's experiences to life, and also to the forefront of your analysis and discussions. Positioning children in this way is representative of their rights to participate and emphasizes the importance of hearing their voices. One approach that is emblematic of these values and compatible with contemporary research with children is feminism.

## Methodological Feature: Feminism

Dickson-Swift, James and Liamputtong (2008) argue that qualitative research viewed from an interpretivist perspective is an excellent approach for feminist researchers to take, as it enhances their understanding of people and their experiences. Feminist philosophical perspectives underpin a great deal of our own research. These methodological values require ideas to be collaborative between researcher and participant. Equally, the importance of building nurturing, reciprocal relationships, which focus on the well-being and care of participants is central. You may note that such qualities are also integral to research with children.

---

### ACTIVITY 2.11
Read around the topic of feminist research.
- Identify definitions of qualitative research and its central tenets.
- Write a paragraph that puts these ideas into your own words.
- Consider the implications of this approach for your own methodology.

---

In writing about these philosophies, you have begun to assemble your methodological approach. The methodological features presented here are not meant as a prescription and clearly there are many other possibilities that you may wish to include or prioritize for your own study. Notwithstanding alternative inclusions/exclusions, here you have a basis for a solid and trustworthy foundation on which to situate your research. In other words, you have identified and collected a set of complimentary ingredients for your chosen methodological cake.

## Methodology and Me

As you will have discovered already in this chapter, your methodology will be influenced by your ideas about children and childhood and your own personal experiences, as well as your wider reading and interests. Therefore, these connections between your research interests and who you are in everyday life become central to the underpinning of your methodology and all the following aspects of your dissertation. The methodological choices you make therefore reveal a great deal about your research but even more perhaps about you as a person.

After spending years, disregarding the inclusion of self in their work, due to its argued connotations with 'bias', students can find the promotion of self, challenging. With its links to unfairness, preference and partiality, the avoidance of bias calls researchers to step back from their studies and identities and be more detached, neutral and objective. These ideas, however, as you can now acknowledge belong to a different voice, perspective and methodology. From within our qualitative, interpretivist and feminist framework, the self and its tangible connections with our own research are not something to be ignored but rather something to be acknowledged as a strength in our research, and reflexively considered. Who you are holds up a mirror to all aspects of your study from the title to the aims, to the methodology, methods, ethics and the way the work is presented and written up. Whatever else a methodology might be, you can now recognize that it harmonizes with your values and beliefs and complements the methods and approaches you take. Your methodology is you.

## Our/Your Research Methodology

The final section of this chapter aims to bring together our methodological discussions thus far by providing you with the opportunity to weave together your own individual methodological narrative. To do this, we ask you to first examine activity 2.12 in which we present our methodological approach to a piece of research we conducted with young children. Perhaps drawing on this example, we then ask you to take some time to consider activity 2.13 from which you can begin to formulate and develop your own ideas for the content and features of your methodological approach.

> ### ACTIVITY 2.12
> This research took place in the playground of a primary school with children aged four and five years. The playground happened to also be a disused graveyard, complete with gravestones and memorials. As researchers we wanted to understand the children's perceptions of this play space.
> - Take some time to consider the above scenario and how you, as a researcher, might move forward with this.
> - Identify the key methodological concepts and values, which should privilege the perceptions of these young participants.
> - What methods might you use to elicit the children's views?
> - Now read our methodological account, referenced here and see if your ideas are similar to ours: Coombs, S. and Richards, S. 'A Bump on the Head in the Graveyard: Palimpsests of Death, Selves, Care and Touch', in Richards, S. and Coombs, S. (2023) (Eds) *Critical Perspectives in Research with Children: Reflexivity, Methodology and Researcher Identity*, Bristol: Bristol University Press, p. 138–56.
> - Consider which concepts might be relevant to include in your methodology.

> **ACTIVITY 2.13**
> Considering all the discussions we have shared together in this chapter the time is now right for you to put together the features of your own methodology.
> - First, if you have not already done so, then identify a topic that you would like to explore with children.
> - Develop or review your aim and objectives.
> - Write your definition of the term 'methodology' and its significance in your research.
> - Review methodological values, beliefs and philosophical standpoint/s in this chapter and from your wider reading. Then list the concepts that will form the basis of your methodology. Remember, these are the ingredients that will make your methodological cake.
> - Using your chosen concepts, values and beliefs expand on each to construct a coherent methodological narrative of your own.
> - Identify what methods you will use to compliment your methodology and help you achieve your aim.
> - Finally, recognize both the difference and the relationship between your methodology and methods.

## Conclusion

Perhaps you began this chapter unsure of what a methodology is. We hope that you leave it with the knowledge and confidence to identify and assemble the key methodological features of your own study. We anticipate that the activities within the chapter have helped you to identify and combine some values, beliefs and philosophical ideas, which can contribute to your understanding of methodology, and their relevance to your own principles and practices of research with children. The potential for a clear pathway through the methodological maze should now be visible. What may have appeared initially intimidating should now seem more approachable, culminating in your own mix of perspectives, which when blended, offer up a sound methodological foundation. This way-of-seeing illuminates the interconnected nature of methodology with all the other aspects of your dissertation.

Most importantly perhaps, you now have a heightened awareness of yourself in the construction of this methodology and your overall research project. It took us a long time to realize that we would not find a ready-made methodology in a book, but rather we would need to locate methodological ideas and values from across many forms of literature, and equally it was our responsibility to choose the ones that spoke to us, mix them together and see ourselves in the result. It takes a while to develop this level of confidence, but over the many years of supervising dissertations we have seen students do just that, and their voices become clearly identifiable in their writing. The process, we contend, begins with an understanding and then application of methodological thinking. Our aim for this chapter was to help you with both of these key components.

# 3

# Considering Child-Centred Research

## Introduction

In recent decades, research that claims to place children at the centre of enquiry has been positioned as the ideal, and often, as an ethically superior way to conduct research. This focus on the agentic voice and participation of the child can be traced to the United Nations Convention on the Rights of the Child (1989) and the emergence of the 'new' sociology of childhood in the 1980s/1990s. Child-centred research now dominates the field of childhood studies to such an extent that seeking the voice of the child is generally regarded as evidence of ethical research that gathers an authentic understanding of childhood and children's lives. We certainly do not argue against the notion of research that values children's perspectives. Rather here, as elsewhere (Clark and Richards 2017), we suggest that it is the interrogation of such assumptions that is vital to the production of valid data, ethical approaches, and good quality research relationships grounded in care and trust (Coombs and Richards 2023). For example, in this chapter we question if the non-participating child is problematic or empowered; are we, as adults, always the powerful ones in the research encounter; and when seeking the voice of the child are we paying sufficient attention to the embedded context in which such data is produced?

To this end, the chapter offers an examination of the rise of child-centred participation and the continuum on which it sits. Furthermore, it illustrates ways in which you can critically engage with key concepts central to child participatory methodologies, such as agency, participation and voice, and interrogate these as you deploy them throughout your own research project. You will find activities throughout this chapter, which are designed to provide you with content that can be used directly in your dissertation to evaluate your choice of methodology, and reflexively consider your application of key ideas such as child-centred research. The purpose of this chapter therefore is to help you interrogate the fundamental ideas associated with child-centred research.

## The Rise of Child-Centred Approaches

Research in the broader social sciences underwent a shift in the latter half of the twentieth century. This qualitative turn moved away from deductive, arguably reductive, explanations towards a more interpretive and situated search for meaning. Denzin and Lincoln (2008: vii) suggest:

> For nearly four decades, a quiet methodological revolution has been taking place in the social sciences. A blurring of disciplinary boundaries has occurred. The social sciences and humanities have drawn closer together in a mutual focus on an interpretive, qualitative approach to inquiry, research and theory. Although these trends are not new, the extent to which the 'qualitative revolution' has taken over the social sciences and related professional fields continues to be nothing short of amazing.

This paradigm shift increased the popularity of interpretivist methodologies, for example feminism and symbolic interactionism, and their associated methods, such as unstructured interviews, focus groups and participant observation. The overarching aim of much of this research was to hear the views of previously neglected, hidden, silenced or marginalized groups. Such a reorientation is identifiable across a range of publications and scholarship, for example Becker (1967) *Whose Side Are We On?*; Hall, Critcher, Jefferson, Clarke and Roberts (1978) *Policing the Crisis: Mugging, the State and Law and Order*; Hebdige (1979) *Subculture: The Meaning of Style*, also the development of symbolic interactionism associated with the Chicago School in the early twentieth century, the rise of feminist scholarship (e.g. see Stanley and Wise 1993) and disability studies (e.g. see Shakespeare 2006).

Research with children has also undergone a similar transformation. Historically, childhood enquiry was dominated by particular sub-disciplinary silos such as developmental psychology, psychoanalysis and the sociology of education. Within such domains theoretical analysis of childhood was often limited to adult perspectives only, in which the measurement of educational performance, behaviour and standardized development took priority. You will, of course, be well acquainted with Piaget's theories of child development, Burman (2008) arguing that no nurse, teacher, social worker or counsellor will have completed their training without learning these influential ideas. Here, we add students of childhood studies. Yet, James, Jenks and Prout (1998: 17) argue that these theories produced the most 'materially reductive' image of childhood that we are ever likely to encounter. Similarly, Jenks (1996: 25) envisions the child as 'abandoned to theory', 'the violence of ... scientific rationality', and the 'tyrannical realm of fact' at the expense of the social context. Such linear models of maturation, combined with philosophies of innocence, unknowingness and irrationality, produce a picture of 'the child' as vulnerable and dependent. Children were thus constructed as objects of concern rather than persons with voice (Hallett and Prout 2003), their ultimate task being to develop, mature and become an adult.

However, from the 1970s onwards, in many Western cultures, a powerful and persuasive rights discourse swept through the social institutions of childhood (Clark and Richards 2017). This new sociology of childhood, originally championed by the likes of Alanen (1988), Corsaro (1997) and James, Jenks and Prout (1998), argued for children as active, agentic beings in their present state, and not just the autonomous, adult, neoliberal citizen they were 'ideally' projected to become. Previous assumptions that children could not speak for themselves were questioned, and arguably, subsequent voices have been taken more seriously. Mayall (2002) claimed that in order to learn about the lives of children then research must centre on the child's point of view rather than approaches that spoke for children, effectively silencing them. Thus, this new sociology began to call into question the privileging of adult views of children and childhood, and principles of children's participation, agency and voice became rallying cries for the contemporary social study of children.

The idea that children had something valuable to offer in research expanded the focus of research beyond the previously mentioned educationalism, developmentalism and generalized predictions of progression. Hitherto ignored themes such as children's experiences of their social worlds became valuable and relevant to our understanding of the plurality of childhoods, rather than seeking generalizable models through which childhoods could be organized. Therefore, just as feminism opened a variety of insights into the everyday lives of women, so too did these new areas of childhood research expose previously unknown aspects of children's lives.

Prout (2005: 7) suggests that 'traditional ways of representing childhood no longer seem adequate to its emerging forms'. The onus, therefore, is on researchers to continually challenge and extend the continuum on which research with children sits; thus, seeking to bring children and their experiences to the forefront of discussions. Reductive and outmoded notions of childhood positioned children as passive *becomings*, the powerless recipients of societal/adult norms, traditions and knowledge. More recent discussions place children on a scale from active, agentic *beings*, to experts in their own lives.

In turn, novel ways of regarding children and childhoods prompted significant developments in the participatory methods and methodologies required to facilitate the gathering of agentic voices and bring them to prominence. Method development and selection now focus on seeking effective ways to ensure the participation of children, for example ethnographic approaches (Montgomery 2007), collecting stories (Richards 2012), focus groups (Zonio 2017) and pictures and drawings (McTague, Froyum and Risman 2017). Such innovative approaches deserve to be celebrated for furthering the inclusion of children in research in more varied and meaningful ways. However, it is important to note that the adoption of child-centred methods does not necessarily mean that a child's voice will be effectively heard.

Arguably, the gathering of children's views, though not problematic in itself, became overly reliant on mostly uncontested and uninterrogated notions of children's agency, participation and voice. Consequently, our often-comfortable assumptions as researchers about our abilities to illustrate and shed light on the lives of children can remain relatively unchallenged. However, here we argue that difficult questions should be asked in relation to authenticity of voices, the role and fluidity of power in the research encounter, and indeed, whether children's voices are always ideal or even necessary (Philo 2011). Exposing such debates in research discussions enables us to interrogate the validity of child-centred claims and thereby expose tokenistic notions of participation and explore the ethical dilemmas that such methodologies can generate. It is debates such as these that should be evidenced in your dissertation.

# The Continuum of Child-Centred Research

Children's participation in research, and other aspects of their lives, exists on a continuum. Hart's ladder of participation (Hart 1992) is a useful tool here, where children's rights, voices and input can be seen to vary depending on context and approach. Hart presents a range of involvement that extends from a complete lack of consultation to the gathering of children's views, and onto the full inclusion of children in all aspects of a project or piece of research. In the latter case, children are argued to be sufficiently empowered to take on the role of researchers themselves, and thus involved in all aspects of research from design, method selection, data collection, analysis and dissemination of findings. Some argue that enabling children to be researchers is the ultimate goal in conducting child-centred research, which can produce the most authentic understandings of their lives (Cheney 2011). Others, however, contest this stance, arguing that being a professional researcher encompasses learned, specialist skills that are inappropriate to expect in non-expert children or adults (Hammersley 2015). Therefore, involving children to this extent is not an automatic route to ethically superior research or more valid data. There is no universal place on this continuum that can always be labelled good or bad, much will depend on the research question, methodology and method. However, if you wish to claim your research is child-centred then considering where it sits on this continuum is a useful first point to begin reflection and evaluation. Activity 3.1 is provided to assist you in this.

---

**ACTIVITY 3.1**

You might consider your research to be child-centred, however, it is not sufficient to simply state this, you must interrogate why and how.

- First, examine Hart's *Ladder of Participation*, available on page 8 of the reference provided. See Hart, R. A. (1992) *Children's Participation: From Tokenism to Citizenship*, Innocenti Essay, no. 4, International Child Development Centre, Florence. Available at https://www.unicef-irc.org/publications/100-childrens-participation-from-tokenism-to-citizenship.html
- Consider which rung of the ladder your project sits on.
- How would you justify or defend your decision? For example, is it the methods you have chosen, the role/s children play in your project, the ways in which children are situated within your methodology, or all of these?

---

It is often assumed that a higher position on Hart's ladder equals better, more valid and more ethical research. However, we suggest that positioning children in supposedly more central or powerful roles in the research process does not automatically amount to 'better' research. We are not arguing for the dismissal of children's voices, and equally, share remaining concerns that contemporary research has yet to go far enough. Horgan (2017: 256) argues that 'child participatory research has much potential which has not yet been mined and attending to ... [this] has the potential to contribute to "deeper participation"'. The continued marginalization of disabled children's perspectives (Boggis 2011), the stubborn persistence of assent instead of informed consent (Richards, Clark and Boggis 2015) and topics which remain taboo by virtue of adult fear as opposed to children's competence (Coombs 2014, 2017) remain stubborn examples of this.

After decades of child-centred methodology it would be easy to assume children's expertise. However, is such an assumption valid? Do children have any more authority in shaping their lives now than they did before child-centred research came to dominate the landscape? Do children have more power, and do their perspectives change the organizations in which children are situated? Do the key concepts of child-centred research, agency, voice and participation elevate the status of children beyond the research projects in which they sit? How then do we explore the realities of these key concepts in the research process, which might in turn lead to more tangible outcomes for children? These questions are increasingly interrogated in contemporary research with children, perhaps indicative of the dynamic nature of this type of research and emblematic of where your project may sit.

## Critiquing Agency, Voice and Participation

Research with children is arguably focused on three preoccupations, that is, the canonical concepts of voice, agency and participation. Whilst the ideological underpinning of these concepts has, and continues to promise, firm foundations for new, vital and groundbreaking research, the time is right to explore such notions more critically. You will undoubtedly find a wealth of literature that supports the participation of children in research, calls upon us to listen to their authentic voices and promotes their agency and competency, you will need to familiarize yourself with such fundamental discussions. We now explore the different ways in which you can claim and critique child-centred research within your dissertation. Such discussions can help to demonstrate your critical knowledge and understanding and thus elevate your research-based discussions.

## Voice?

As previously discussed, children have traditionally been constructed as objects of research, and their first-hand accounts considered largely unimportant. Indeed Mayes (2019: 1196) contends that in establishing predominantly psychological, medical and linguistic patterns of child development that the 'voice has been detached from the body of the child – objectified, extracted and analysed by the allegedly-distanced researcher'. However, changes across the social sciences, and in particular childhood studies, have critiqued such approaches and recognized the potential of engaging with and listening directly to others. As Mayes (2019: 1196) asserts, 'This analytical move sought to return voice back to the speaking subject of research.' Therefore, the transformation of children into competent social actors, supposed that, through their own words, children could provide valuable insights into their own lives and what it means to be a child. Childhood studies embraced this notion of 'voice', to such an extent, that Spyrou (2011: 151) claims 'the interdisciplinary field of childhood studies has built its very raison d'etre around the notion of children's voice'.

The promise of children's 'voice' has been extensive; authenticity of voice, first-hand accounts, more equal power relationships, insights into children's experiences, revelations of previously unknown knowledge, the possibility for children's greater participation in organizations and deeper understanding of children's lives. The enthusiasm for the notion of voice or as Cooper (2023: 1) contends, 'A focus on an individualised approach to "giving voice" to children has resulted in a large body of participatory research' [examples given in original]. As childhood researchers ourselves, we frequently employ the notion of voice in our attempts to listen to children and facilitate conversations on a range of subjects. Both philosophically and practically we find the idea of children's voice enticing, with all its hopes and possibilities. We endorse the values of children's participation in research, listening to their viewpoints, being present as perspectives are discussed, constructed, reconstructed and deconstructed by the young people around us, we recognize their expertise and aim to bring their views to the forefront of discussions. And yet, do we? In our interpretations whose voice are we actually hearing? Can the reality of 'voice' live up to the rhetoric presented?

Richards, Clark and Boggis (2015) explore the limitations of voice, questioning the ethical positions of those who claim to represent the voices of others, their interpretation of personal accounts and their choices in de/selecting data. They contend that through such processes it is conventional voices that are privileged over those less easily accessed and heard. The hegemonic notion of voice is therefore rendered contentious in its hierarchical elevation of particular voices and marginalization of others. Critiques of childhood voice extend further, interrogating its erasure of difference, its appropriation of other and its uncritical representation of children's voices without questioning the complexity of context in which they were produced (see Mayes 2019: 1196 for full arguments). Mayes (2019: 1197) argues that researchers should be more aware of 'the situated, partial and particular nature of voices, not to take responses as unwavering truth, or to assume that "giving voice" is the pathway to the authentic, core being'. Without consideration of such rich entanglements, Mayes (2019: 1197) goes on to suggest that '[d]iscursive violence may be done in the name of dialogue and participatory research; in the research event, speech may still remain within the bounds of what the researcher can hear'.

Despite some of the discussions above, we would nevertheless encourage you to seek the voices of children in your research projects. This remains a very worthwhile endeavour but should be undertaken with the knowledge of its limitations, and a recognition of the impact on the voices used in your research, including your own.

---

**ACTIVITY 3.2**

Bearing in mind the discussions of 'voice' presented in this section.
- Identify and outline the historical influences, current arguments and evaluations, and the strengths and limitations of this concept.

---

## Agency?

Seeking children's views and perspectives is premised on a theoretical assumption, grounded in the new sociology of childhood, that children have agency. That is to say that children hold some power to make decisions about their lives and generate action. While debates around agency and empowering or limiting structures have raged in the social sciences for decades, childhood studies has not yet fully engaged in an active, critical interrogation of such ideas and concepts, to the same degree as other fields. Feminism has challenged such terms as agency and autonomy, for example Isaacs (2002: 129) argues that traditional conceptions of agency are 'overly individualistic and valorise an illusory and unattractive ideal of agents and agency'. Similarly, disability studies has embraced post-human perspectives in order to interrogate the notion of humanity and humanness, and its implications for dis/abled bodied persons and their everyday agency (Goodley and Runswick-Cole 2016). The term 'agency' is often adopted in research with children, with method selection predicated upon the assumption of the individual child as being active, autonomous, agentic and having a voice. These concepts can be seen as deeply embedded in contemporary neoliberal cultures where the rational, autonomous and individualized citizen is prized.

The rise of post-structural and post-human perspectives questions the ideal hierarchical position of the 'human' and increasingly leans towards the scrutiny of interdependent and intergenerational relationships. Thus, prompting a critique of agency as only understood in an individualized, neoliberal sense. An appreciation of the social and relational aspects of agency allows us to recognize the collaborative and context bound nature of decision-making, voice and meaning-making. This has implications for your selection of method. Traditional ideas of individual agency may be promoted through the use of questionnaires or surveys, which would seem ideal to gain an authentic, objective and anonymous understanding of young people's views and agency. However, if agency is conceptualized both in social terms and relationally then methods which facilitate social exchange, such as participant observation or focus groups, may be preferable. While this acknowledgement of co-construction seems problematic for some, perhaps because it threatens the sanctity of the individual voice of the child, it has the potential to better reflect how children, and indeed adults, understand and express themselves in the world. Therefore, the method you select will be in part determined by your definition of agency and will subsequently reproduce and confirm that definition. We hope activity 3.3 will help you identify these different characterizations of agency and your subsequent choice of methods.

### ACTIVITY 3.3
Consider these two alternative constructions of agency. That is, agency defined in individualized, neoliberal terms and agency defined in terms of being relational, social, interconnected and embedded with others.
- Identify different methods of data collection you could use that articulate these perspectives and why.
- Consider how you might realize and articulate one of these through your choice of method.

While activity 3.3 asks you to consider how you are defining agency and its role in shaping your research method, it equally determines how you will present agency throughout your methodology section.

In the field, children's agency can emerge in unexpected, creative and imaginative ways. Dissertation students have sometimes come to us concerned about the limited numbers of children willing to take part in their research. We encourage students to recognize the ways in which, as a researcher, they have enabled a child, often within an educational setting, to say no. The capacity for a child to say no, within an educational context is not to be underestimated. Such experiences are therefore not necessarily evidence of non-engagement in research but rather a child who feels comfortable, or at least able, often in hierarchical circumstances, to dissent.

An example of unexpected, or even unwanted agency, is represented in the following example. A dissertation student was concerned that the children in her focus group only wanted to talk about *ChildLine* when the research topic was, in fact, about friendships. However, on listening to the data more closely, it became clear that the children were indeed talking about friendships, covering aspects of care, respect, feelings of happiness, and notions of being kind and having someone to talk too. This was not, as the student feared, lost data but rather, a fine example of children's thoughtfulness, creative expression and their agency in guiding the research encounter. Children present their agency in many ways, and if you have already collected your data from children or if you work with children in an educational capacity, you may have experienced this. Activity 3.4 helps you to reflect on such experiences.

### ACTIVITY 3.4
Identify examples of children's agency in your research project or daily interactions with children and consider the following:
- Did data collection with the children happen as you anticipated? Were there any unexpected events, conversations or happenings?
- Were there any moments when you felt out of control in the conversations or activities with the children? Why was this? What had been said or done? What data was produced in this moment?

How we understand concepts such as agency shapes how we both design research and respond in the field. Being reflexive about our status, research relationships and preconceived theoretical ideas support greater interrogation of agency in childhood. Children who choose to say 'no' are not necessarily disempowered, children who construct views with peers have not necessarily been led off topic, and the conversations that children have as relational, rather than individual participants, remain agentic despite their collaborative context.

---

**ACTIVITY 3.5**
Bearing in mind the discussions of 'agency' presented in this section.
- Identify and outline the historical influences, current arguments and evaluations, and the strengths and limitations of this concept.
- Consider how you might realize and articulate these discussions in your dissertation.

---

## Participation?

In the same way that voice and agency became central tenets of research with children, so too participation. Once we assume that children are agentic beings we endow them with a degree of competence, thus their voices become worthy of attention, and their participation is sought after. Just as the notion of children's voice was referred to earlier as the 'raison d'etre' (Spyrou 2011) on which the field of childhood studies was built, so too has participation been positioned as the 'sine qua non', that is, something indispensable or essential (Roberts 2008: 273). More recently, Clark and Richards (2017: 130) describe how child participation has become a 'normative mantra', received as 'ethically superior' in its production of more valid research.

Ideas of children's participation arose from beliefs and expectations that children should become more involved in their schools, families and wider communities. Such notions emerged from the wider neoliberal agenda that requires adults to participate in society as independent, individualized social actors, thus necessitating that children also acquire such skills (Clark and Richards 2017). Participation is frequently construed as a right in childhood but may also be seen as an obligation, where children are made responsible or even compelled to take part, so as to attain the skills of future citizenship (Raby 2014). For example, examine critiques surrounding children's membership of school councils, where children's participation is often expected and yet regarded in tokenistic ways.

Similar arguments can be applied to the ways in which participation is realized in research. The original promise of participation was premised on children's capabilities and their right to take part. We support these assertions while maintaining that such discussions should include both the promises and limitations of child engagement. For example, it was envisioned that involvement would transform the lives of participating children, but has it? One argument is that children benefit through the changes generated by their participation. However, such tangible benefits remain, too often, elusive, and young people can now be reluctant to engage in research or consultation processes as they see little change in their circumstances (Tyrell 2023). Furthermore, it is often the topics that fascinate us as adults that are on offer to children, and arguably may be of little, or no, interest to them. Similarly, adult researchers and society more generally often consider some topics to be appropriate to discuss with children and others to be totally off limits, thereby restricting their participation. This discrepancy is highlighted by Uprichard (2010: 7), who suggests that children should be involved in projects that extend beyond the traditional spaces of childhood, that is, 'children are capable of talking about many, many things, not just about their childhood lives'. Uprichard (2010) questions the narrow ways in which children are called to participate in research, which continue to focus solely on their lives and experiences in childhood. True participation, she argues, can only occur when researchers extend their remit to include children in projects beyond the confines of accepted and conventional realms of childhood. We concur with Uprichard's claim but suggest there is now increasing evidence of children's inclusion across a wider range of topics. See, for example, Rawat (2023) as she discusses children's experiences of parental sex workers in India. Similarly, Coombs (2017) broadens the concept of participation in her exploration of social aspects of death with young people, a topic often considered taboo for adult conversation, let alone children.

Not only does such research expand the involvement of children into sensitive topics but also extends the meaning of participation (Coombs 2017). Here, she situates the young people as 'accomplished participants' and 'pioneers' of this sensitive research project (Coombs 2017: 197). Equally she claims that the language of being a participant may perpetuate outmoded constructions of children as passive contributors, whereas a pioneer has strengths, such as adventurering, inventing and discovering. Concepts such as participant and pioneer continue to develop, change and evolve, as new researchers re-define these terms in their work. Whilst children may not directly benefit from their involvement in such research, having their insights into these topics both enriches and expands everyone's knowledge and understanding.

Child-friendly, participatory methods are largely recognized as the gold standard for eliciting children's participation. However, these are not without critique. As researchers we spend a great deal of our time creating specific methods, which we hope children will enjoy and will enable their involvement. We go to great lengths to facilitate drawings, paintings, collages, photographs, map-making, online methods, guided tours, focus groups, friendship groups and so on. Yet there are those who oppose the need for alternative and specific methods for children. Punch (2002), for example, claims that adults may also like to use such methods.

One of the arguments for the use of distinctive methods in childhood research is that they support the equalization of power imbalances often inherent between adult researcher and child participant. However, this oft-repeated discussion also requires examination. Adult researchers often attempt to become 'less than' a researcher in order to balance the relationships within these encounters. They may position themselves as 'adult friend' or a 'different type of adult' (Christiansen 2004: 174) or they may refer to participants as 'co-researchers' (Canosa, Graham and Wilson 2018: 403). Alternatively, as Canosa, Graham and Wilson (2018) argue, whilst striving to be the 'adult friend' it may be necessary to become the 'adult in control' and assert authority. Clearly, participatory research is a continuous balancing act between such positions. We suggest that it might only be in the moments when we, rather frighteningly, begin to lose control of research situations in practice that our rigid preoccupations with theoretical and academic concepts momentarily vanish. It is then, that we perhaps see the true participation of children and often under such circumstances we close the vision very quickly for fear of what it shows us. For example, see Coombs and Richards (2023) as they carry out a research project with young children who soundly assert their choice to play rather than engage in the research. A further example occurred when one of our students, using a focus group, was attempting to collect data on children's citizenship during the first snowfall of the year. Thus, she only gathered data on snow, as the children were so excited and preoccupied.

The realities of children's engagement can often mean that research plans and expectations flounder. In the face of actual engagement with children, we often find that researchers have less control than anticipated. This reveals a quandary in which we seek participation but only in a form that enables the researcher to retain control. Arguably, therefore, the adult world, despite its protestations to the contrary, may not be ready for the true participation of children and perhaps subsequently neither are we as researchers. However, despite concerns surrounding a neoliberal agenda, the rhetoric of participation, and pertinent questions regarding the benefits of engagement, children's participation should and does continue to be constructed as emancipatory.

> **ACTIVITY 3.6**
> Bearing in mind the discussions of 'participation' presented in this section.
> - Identify and outline the historical influences, current arguments and evaluations, and the strengths and limitations of this concept.
> - Consider how you might realize and articulate these discussions in your dissertation.

# Situating Voice, Agency and Participation in Context

The idea of including children in research was very much centred on the recognition of the *being* child, bestowed with abilities hitherto ignored. In research, these qualities are dominated by such features as voice, agency and participation. Debates and discussions are therefore centred on deconstructed characteristics of children rather than recognizing the whole child. Focusing on such individual aspects encourages children's voices to be extracted, disembodied and thereby separated from not only the child, but also the context in which they were produced. Such arguments can similarly be extended into the ways in which agency and participation are articulated within research. In our pursuit of the being child, we have somehow lost the recognition of the social child. Thus, their capacity to identify hierarchies, recognize the emotional needs of others and their skills as social actors are often neglected in research discussions. We need to re-embed this child back into the social context to reveal their entanglements with social interactions, materiality and environments. Through the appreciation of children as social actors in specific contexts we realize their agency and participation and hear their voice. As part of research discussions, we should embrace, rather than ignore the rich contexts and situatedness in which these concepts emerge.

Activity 3.7 allows you to reflect on these important contextual details.

> **ACTIVITY 3.7**
> Consider the following scenarios of data collection. Reflect upon the importance of providing contextual details to situate and better understand children's voices and actions.
> - Consider children in the context of a focus group. What role might friendships play with regard to the children's voices, silences and co-constructed ideas?
> - Why might it be important to include these details in your discussions and findings?
> - How do such debates advance your understanding of agency, voice and participation?
> - Alternatively, consider research in a classroom setting. How might the proximity of the teacher be shaping the ways in which children behave (agency), respond (voice) and interact (participation)?
> - What benefits does adding the context have for your research discussions?

# Conclusion

This chapter has illustrated the emergence of child-centred research and the promises it brought. Our aim was to provide content that supports you in building details on the origins of child-centred research. We also provide opportunities for critical evaluation of key concepts, and to encourage you to recognize the importance of situating these in children's everyday lives and the social environments in which they live. The activities embedded within this chapter should help you to demonstrate a more critical knowledge and understanding of the central tenets, on which, participatory research with children is built.

# 4

# Utilizing Key Concepts

## Introduction

This chapter aims to explore valuable qualitative research concepts which, when applied throughout your dissertation, bring recognition and scrutiny of the self to the fore. Concepts, such as subjectivity, positionality, reflexivity and others, which we will examine throughout this chapter, often appear distant from ourselves and our work but nothing could be further from the truth. Such outlooks ultimately encourage us to be critically inclusive of the self in all our research endeavours. We only need to grasp this, to recognize the opportunities that such notions provide us with, to acknowledge and interrogate our own specific place or places in our work.

Undergraduate/postgraduate researchers researchers can often neglect to account for their own presence in their research projects and, in addition, the influences that their identities, subjectivities and relationships have in their fieldwork. Initially, as part of the ethics application, students are usually encouraged to, at least, consider research relationships but mostly as potential contaminants to the production of authentic, valid and legitimate knowledge. Often unacknowledged in this process are the ways in which researchers and participants share commonalities of experience and/or professional roles, which are used in the collection of data either implicitly or explicitly. Research relationships are developed in, and inform all aspects of, the research journey, and yet are commonly neglected in subsequent analysis and discussions.

This chapter extends the relational debate to move beyond rudimentary disclosures on an ethics form and asks students to consider the ways in which who they are shapes what they find, and why they find it. Using a variety of concepts, such as positionality, self-disclosure, category entitlement, subjectivity and reflexivity, facilitates recognition and analysis of the integral role of researcher identity and their relationships in the construction of knowledge. Here, we clarify these research concepts and outline how students can use them to account for the ways in which such relationships influence their data. We provide examples of their use and demonstrate how the 'problem' of research relationships can become an opportunity for greater knowledge and understanding of the complexities of social research.

In this chapter, we outline ways in which you, as an individual, can be acknowledged and accounted for in your research. Doing so should not be regarded as a self-centred vanity project but rather part of the ongoing debates that make qualitative approaches to research so rich and contextualized. Here, the contested and sometimes controversial position(s) of the researcher are made evident. To achieve this aim, we outline three connected, yet separate concepts: positionality, category entitlement and self-disclosure. Indeed, we have highlighted and explored these themes elsewhere (see Richards, Clark and Boggis 2015; Richards and Coombs 2023) but the focus here is on enabling you to recognize and utilize them as significant features in your research. First however, a word of caution, being too focused on our own presence is not necessarily regarded as particularly appropriate and can be considered as somewhat egotistical (Atkinson and Coffey 2003; Lyttle-Storrod 2023), or even potentially professionally risky (Sanchez-Taylor and Davidson 2010). It can also be a distraction from the focus of your dissertation but to ignore or reject our positions and their potential impact on our research is both illusionary and somewhat duplicitous. We also warn that recognizing the presence and extent of our influence is not necessarily straightforward but our identities, and those of our participants, are central to the research produced and should be acknowledged as such.

Our intention for this chapter is to make the concepts mentioned in this introduction accessible, and therefore available for you to employ within your research. We provide examples throughout the chapter of how you might incorporate these ideas, and by so doing, extend and enrich your dissertation discussions. We begin by examining two centrally important concepts, that is, subjectivity and reflexivity, from which the other pivotal concepts will emerge.

## Subjectivity and Reflexivity

Prior to focusing on the particularities of positionality, category membership and self-disclosure, we first need to familiarize you with two highly pertinent and useful concepts, that is, subjectivity and reflexivity. Developing an understanding of both offers you great opportunities for critical and immersive reflection in your dissertation.

We begin with subjectivity, which can be broadly described as the involvement and acknowledgement of the researcher in all aspects of the research process. Dickson-Swift, James and Liamputtong (2008: 22) argue that 'qualitative research is a subjective experience' and that 'researchers cannot hide behind the mask of objectivity and pretend they are not intimately involved in the research that they do'. A subjective stance is clearly in stark contrast to an objective position that seeks to maintain an adequate, even extensive, distance from participants, by excluding the researcher's presence from their work and attempting to eliminate all vestiges of personal bias. Contrary to the subjectivity of qualitative research, quantitative researchers have often pursued overarching grand narratives and/or universal truths, via attempts at absolute objectivity and positivist approaches. However, even these methodologies are being encouraged to question if the tools of positivism are still appropriate. The quantitative researcher, Grbich (2004: 28) argues, 'must become a more participatory being', embracing 'multiple hypotheses', 'lack of control' and 'the incorporation of descriptive, subjective information'.

Rather than expecting the researcher to step out of their research and be objective, instead subjectivity encourages the researcher to step in and acknowledge their presence. In this way, the researcher cannot be a remote, nameless and faceless director of their research; rather, they must acknowledge their subjective involvements in daily life and in their research relationships and data collection. Subjectivity then is individual to each researcher, and each topic, and subsequently no two applications of subjectivity will look the same. For example, when Sarah chose to research children's everyday perceptions of death, it was her own previous experiences, both personal and professional, which were openly acknowledged. The sharing of her personal involvements, her singular thoughts, feelings and perceptions, provided insights into the individual context of this research and the decisions made throughout the project. Consequently, Sarah was and is firmly situated as an insider in her work. Now, look at activity 4.1 and consider aspects of your own subjective involvement in your dissertation project.

---

**ACTIVITY 4.1**

If, as argued, qualitative research is a subjective experience and calls us to acknowledge our own subjective involvement in our work, then ...
- Contemplate your own relationships with your chosen topic.
- Consider the difficulties you might face if you try and filter yourself out of our research project.

---

The acknowledgement of subjective influences in our work enables researchers from this perspective to recognize more readily the countless many truths that transpire from our own subjectivities and those of our participants.

It is within this context of these plural truths that your dissertation can sit. Grbich (2004: 28) suggests that 'subjectivity becomes paramount' in a place, where multiple views, truths and identities are accepted, and where no voice is privileged above another. Within this paradigm, your subjectivity is encouraged to be made apparent, rather than hidden. Indeed, Ryan-Flood and Gill (2010: 1) argue that such research demands that 'the unseen and the unacknowledged be made visible and heard'. This openness should be acknowledged as a strength within your research, although such directness can often feel exposing, and consequently attempts can be made to shy away from it (Coombs and Richards 2023). The implications of responding to our subjectivity lead us onwards to being reflexive.

Dickson-Swift, James and Liamputtong (2008: 21) describe that 'openness and reflexivity is paramount in qualitative research … '. Notwithstanding such affirmations, reflexivity is not always a straightforward notion to pin down or easy to define. We have previously described it thus, 'Reflexivity requires the researcher to continually survey themselves as an integrated part of the research landscape and recognise the effect that they have on all aspects of research, through the topics chosen to the questions asked and the knowledge produced' (Richards and Coombs 2023). Therefore, if you wish to account for your subjectivity within your research project, then reflexivity is the mechanism by which you can achieve this.

In practice, being reflexive is not necessarily easy, it often challenges us to scrutinize the entirety of the research process. It asks us to reveal things we may not want to and share experiences we would rather hide away (see Coombs and Richards 2023). It calls upon us to recognize the many different selves we bring to our research and the influences they have on knowledge production (see Rawat 2023). It brings us face to face with emotions we might rather deny (see Lyttle-Storrod 2023; Montgomery 2023), and it encourages us to consider broader, deeper questions regarding children and research, and the influence of the contexts in which they are set (Sinha 2023). A reflexive approach informs every aspect of your research, and therefore can be immersive, vibrant, uncomfortable, emotional and expansive.

Baker (2003: 401) contends that our research endeavours 'are not "time out" from social worlds; rather, they are reflexive descriptions of those worlds'. We are therefore, as Hammersley and Atkinson (1995: 17) contend, not separate from what we study as ' ... there is no way we can escape the social world to study it'. Indeed, they argue that we need to reflexively acknowledge and account for our embeddedness and positions. Ristock and Pennell (1996: 66) comply with this stance and contend that as researchers we should begin our analyses from the personal and indicate the ways in which our personal identities inform and shape our research. Using the process of reflexivity, as researchers we can begin to recognize our positionality as dynamic, situated and context specific. Activity 4.2 gives you the opportunity to see a reflexive discussion about research in practice.

> **ACTIVITY 4.2**
> Use the following reference to explore reflexivity.
> Sanchez Taylor, J. and O'Connell, D. (2010), 'Unknowable Secrets and Golden Silences', in Ryan-Flood, R. and Gill, R. (Eds) *Secrecy and Silence in the Research Process: Feminist Reflections*, 42–53, London: Routledge.
> - Consider how this reflexive account is different from other presentations of findings and analysis that you have come across.

Such reflexive inclusion can be neglected in accounts of published research, which frequently overlook the attributes and characteristics of those who collect data. We take the perspective that all those engaged in research bring their identity characteristics, subjective positions and diverse personal histories to the research process. In other words, our individual biographies are always present. Activity 4.3 encourages you to begin to think reflexively about your own research. Starting from the personal, consider ways in which your own individual experiences might influence the responses of your participants.

> **ACTIVITY 4.3**
> As a researcher, you have been asked to explore children's friendships with a group of children.
> - Consider how your own experiences of friendship might influence your response to, or approach with, participants.
> - How might you use reflexivity as part of your analysis of the data?

Using reflexivity in our discussions exposes how our particular positionalities and identities can infer entitlements on the part of the researcher to ask specific questions about their topic, and to evaluate data through these positions and entitlements. For example, Sarah as an adoptive mother asking other adoptive mothers about their mothering practices; a teaching assistant asking other professionals in education about an education topic; a male early years professional asking other male early years professionals about their practices and experiences.

However, such entitlements are not just restricted to the researcher, they can be constructed by participants, who use them to establish their own legitimacy to provide credible responses on a given topic. For example, as a PhD student engaged in interviewing an intercountry adoptive mother, Sarah realized her participant was performing the role expected of her, that of 'a good intercountry adoptive mother'. The participant shared her experience with Sarah, not just as the interviewee but also as a fellow adoptive mother. Once recognized, this changed the analysis, not only of this interview but all subsequent others, as Sarah realised how significant her position was in shaping the responses of her participants. If Sarah was to remain true to the data and her methodology, it was impossible to exclude this influence (Richards 2013). Therefore, Sarah not only embraced the notion of the interview as a type of performance, in which the interviewee seeks to persuade the interviewer to their perspective but also that individual identities and positionalities were being used to construct knowledge and were therefore inextricable from the analysis of the data. This scenario is an example of how category memberships and entitlements are constructed during an interview and can be reflexively explored in dissertations. Silverman (1993: 114) argues that interviews can make explicit the actual identity construction taking place. Such connections however are often ignored, as researchers seek to ensure distance rather than connection with their interviewees in the name of objectivity. Fine (1994) contends that such objectivity contributes to 'othering' participants. Poindexter (2003), however, extends the idea, claiming that the presence and input of the researcher in shaping, analysing and presenting the narratives in particular ways should be recognized but is rarely acknowledged. Such disregard, Geertz (1973) argues, reduces the epistemological richness, contextuality and 'thickness' of the research.

Next, we will explore the ways in which the positions we hold in society and our daily lives influence our work. Similarly, how the social categories we identify with, such as mother, daughter, teacher, and the complex interweaving of these, may lead to the potential for self-disclosure.

## Positionality

Positionality can be defined as an individual's values, beliefs and worldview (Savin-Baden and Howell Major 2013), as well as the position they hold in relation to a specific research topic or theme. Certain elements of our positionality are culturally attributed, such as nationality or race. Other aspects are more contingent, such as our experiences and personal life history. These positions are subjective and relative. Chiseri-Strater (1996: 119) contends that in our studies of others we learn about the self. Positionality requires that we acknowledge and allow for our views, values and beliefs in relation to the research process, and in the claims we make using this research.

Within qualitative approaches, particularly those which champion feminist methodologies, it is now generally understood that the 'products of participatory research are influenced as much by researchers' participation in the field as they are by their reflections on the data' (Borbasi, Jackson and Wilkes 2005: 494). The influence of 'self' is becoming recognized as fundamental in our fieldwork and in the construction of our situated and contextualized accounts. From this perspective, we are generally acknowledged as being the instruments of our data collection processes. Altheide and Johnson (1994) argue that we should be able to identify and justify how our individual positions shape all the stages of the research process. You should be able to recognize this stance from our earlier chapters where we encouraged you to acknowledge the role of self in the development of your methodology and your ethical framework. From this perspective, as researchers, we are positioned 'in' the field alongside our participants rather than 'of' the field and separate from them (Gubrium and Holstein 1999: 563). As such, we should acknowledge that the experiences we have during our fieldwork will change us as much as our participants (Borbasi, Jackson and Wilkes 2005). We therefore need to be reflexive of our positionality or, as Gubrium and Holstein (1999) argue, demonstrate self-conscious analysis. Mauthner and Doucet (2003: 421) argue that 'the interpersonal, political and institutional contexts in which researchers are embedded' perform a fundamental role in determining the decisions they make in the field. After all, as Denzin (1986: 12) argues, 'interpretive research begins and ends with the biography and self of the researcher'.

Our positionalities, therefore, are not just fixed concepts but dynamic and relational, they shift according to who we are with, the context we are in and the role/s we play. What we are attempting to achieve in participatory methodologies is to form relationships and build connections, through which we can gather data. These relationships are argued to be 'fundamental' (Borbasi, Jackson and Wilkes 2005) and are often characterized by care, nurturance, reciprocity, intimacy and self-disclosure (Tong, 1999). Such rapports are representative of feminist methodologies and in particular a feminist ethic of care (Tronto [1993] 2009). Research relationships, such as these, are 'contingent' (Borbasi et al 2005: 495), not always easy to manage, and often complicated by other identity positions that we, and they, our participants, might hold. For a detailed account of the different identity positions that we held during a particular research encounter, see Coombs and Richards (2023).

Clearly relations between researchers and participants are part of the fieldwork experience, and positioning ourselves socially and emotionally in relation to our participants is part of a reflexive process (Mauthner and Doucet 2003). However, such involvement requires boundaries, where you, as the researcher, do not get so involved with your participants that fieldwork becomes difficult to conduct, interpret and gain insights from. To 'go native' is a recognized aspect of researching in familiar places with people you feel connected to, through either common identity characteristics or growing familiarity as a result of the research process. A position somewhere between over-familiarity and distance, where the voices of your participants remain central and elevated, is the balance to aim for. Lipson (1989: 65) argues that good data is achieved through relationships where the participants trust the researcher and where the researcher recognizes her influence. Hammersley and Atkinson (1995: 112) argue that researchers 'can only strive to be intellectually poised between familiarity and strangeness'. Others perhaps more simply claim that researchers need to be skilled in maintaining the boundary of being both researcher and insider (Taylor 2011) in the social worlds that they study.

It is argued that little is revealed by ignoring how positions of familiarity and difference are constructed and used in our research relationships and subsequent analysis. Reflexivity as a mechanism through which to explore our own positions as researchers can be used as a 'tool with which to check … our personal baggage for presumption and prejudice' (Madden 2010: 22). Such an approach is both a prerequisite and an ongoing process for the researcher to be able to clearly identify, articulate and evaluate their own positionality. Such positioning requires researchers to acknowledge and disclose their own selves to help make explicit subjective influences on their research (Cohen, Manion and Morrison 2011).

Reinharz (1997: 5) expresses how she found the process of reflexivity to be 'transformative'. She categorizes the different selves she identified in her work: research-based selves (researcher, academic, listener); brought selves (mother, woman, wife); situationally created selves (temporary member of a group, worker, friend, exhausted). These various selves, our insights into them and documentation of them, Reinharz suggests, are key to understanding the centrality of the self within our fieldwork and release us from 'the epistemological tensions between unreflexive positivism and navel gazing'. It is through this reflexive process that the self can become a 'key fieldwork tool' (as suggested by Van Maanen, Manning and Miller 1989).

---

**ACTIVITY 4.4**

Using the claims made by Reinharz regarding the positionalities we bring to the research field.
- Consider the positionalities you bring to your research.
- How might these shape the relationships you develop within your fieldwork?
- How might your positionalities influence the way you carry out your research and shape the data you get?

---

These positionalities are productive in research in that, it is argued, they place us within membership groups where we are entitled, or not, to receive specific knowledge (Potter and Wetherell 1987). For example, when Sarah carried out research with children relating to the end of life (Coombs 2014), her recruitment strategy ensured she already had established relationships with some of her young participants. This connection meant that acquaintanceship, friendliness, reciprocity, trust and rapport were already partially established through a more commonly ascribed category membership, that of friends-mum or family friend, rather than researcher. Equally, the young people knew each other, as the focus groups were composed of self-selected friends. Therefore, the research was conducted through these pre-existing memberships. Equally, the relationship allowed certain assumptions to be made by the young people, for instance, that Sarah, who had children the same age as them, would recognize and understand some of their cultural references to contemporary books, films and other media sources. However, when instances arose in which Sarah was clearly not a member and therefore not fully understanding the focus of their conversations, the young people felt happy to laugh, joke and [re]ascribe her to the category of unknowing adult.

Such positions or categories in which we place ourselves or are placed by our participants are instrumental in shaping research relationships and therefore data outcomes. We must recognize and acknowledge these and bring them to the forefront of our discussions, without doing so we risk missing rich, contextual and complex elements in our analysis. To encourage you to start thinking about group memberships to which you may or may not belong, and the way in which they influence social interactions, we ask you to think back to your first days at university. Activity 4.5 moves us from the topic of positionality and into the related concept of category membership and entitlement.

### ACTIVITY 4.5
Reflect on your first day at university.
- You are sitting in a classroom surrounded by strangers with whom you need to connect. How might this common experience of strangeness help you establish relationships?
- Now imagine you arrive two weeks later than everyone else. How would this experience be different and potentially more difficult in establishing relationships?
- Consider how being categorized as a member or a non-member of these groups might shape your interactions with others.

# Category Membership and Entitlement

Potter and Wetherell (1987: 116) contend that societal categories are influential in social research, positioning them as 'principle building blocks'. Such categories are often assumed to be stable and durable, such as daughter, son, mother and father. These social categories often have associated characteristics or attributes. We can also be members of numerous categorical groups at any one time, for example, student and employee.

Perceptions of similarity and difference are a function of social categorization (Oakes, Haslan and Turner 1994) where we identify ourselves as belonging to certain membership groups. Social distance is argued to impede trust and increase a lack of understanding between researcher and participants (Miller and Glassner 1997). The establishing of rapport and nurturance is proposed to reduce such distance and enhance understanding between researcher and participant. Within ethnography, Coffey (1999: 47) draws our attention to issues such as stranger versus friend, and involvement versus detachment, where the position of insider or member in the field can offer some advantages as well as make the researcher's role more complex. Being recognized as belonging to a similar group to your participants, therefore, influences your fieldwork.

---

**ACTIVITY 4.6**

Spend a few moments thinking about the categories to which you currently belong: student, daughter, son, football fan, runner, cat/dog owner.

As a football fan, for example, you may be associated with wearing particular clothes on match days, always attending your team's matches, having a season ticket, socializing with other fans of the team, following matches on TV, internet or radio. If asked by others about football you may speak from this category and be seen through this category by others. Your behaviour and conversation will be understood through this category of football fan.

> - As a student, think about the activities your student union or university provides based on the categorical labels associated with being a 'student'.
> - Select one of your other category memberships (such as friend) and identify the characteristics that are associated with it, and the ways that these attributes are used in your social interactions.

We all carry categorical labels and are attributed to the associated characteristics that confer membership. We use categories to shape and understand our social worlds. However, these structures, though often durable, are not always static, more accurately they are dynamic and modified in each social interaction. Through the process of categorization, we help create the collective groups that we claim membership of (Potter and Wetherell 1987), and we construct the 'realities' or truths associated with them (Hacking 1986). As well as placing ourselves in particular categories we can also be ascribed membership by other more powerful social groups. Consequently, the associated qualities or characteristics of that group become assigned to us. Attributions of this type can sometimes occur to such an extent that our individual opportunities and aspirations can be constrained and make it difficult for us to move beyond them. For example, if we take the category of 'welfare recipient' and consider the negative features attributed to this group by, amongst others, some politicians and tabloid newspapers, the list can be extensive. It might include some of the following punitive characteristics: welfare sponger, lazy, scrounger, feckless, undeserving. Such assigned attributes can be hard to escape no matter how invalid and can be frequently imposed upon a less powerful group in society. Hacking (1986) has previously equated social categories with prisons, in which groups become trapped by attendant characteristics with little or no power to escape them.

However, social categories and our membership of them help us to make sense of each other's behaviour and the social environments in which we live (Baker 2003). They act as repositories for cultural knowledge, and we use them to interpret our social worlds and the actions of those around us (Garfinkel 1967). Our own cultural competence is linked to such categories, and therefore may (or may not) assist the participant and researcher in feeling more trusting, comfortable and confident in the research process (Borbasi et al 2005). Thus, if we place a person in the category of 'teacher', we perhaps feel able to predict and understand their actions towards children. However, if we categorize them as 'predator', then our interpretation of their actions is going to be very different.

One of the first ways you might begin to consider the influence of category entitlement in your own research project is in the subject matter you have selected to focus on. Dissertation students are often drawn to select a topic they have personal experience of or feel connected to through their own personal or professional lives. Such knowledge and/or category entitlement often determines the perspectives we hold within the topics we study. Activity 4.7 encourages you to identify the category memberships associated with your topic and your relationships with them. These are important features because how we position ourselves informs the research we do (Poindexter 2003). You could also use the example topic we have provided here.

---

### ACTIVITY 4.7

Consider your relationship with your selected topic and then attempt the questions below.

If you wish to use our example, you could think about a research topic that explores why people choose to be vegan.

- Identify your position on this topic. (Are you vegan or do you advocate eating meat as part of a healthy diet? These are examples of relevant category memberships, which can be influential in your research and interactions with participants).
- Can you identify any other category memberships, which can be related to this topic, either professional or personal? (Nutritionist, a parent anxious about what their children choose to eat).
- Now, apply category memberships to your chosen topic, and consider the influences they might have.

Category entitlement can also be influential in your recruitment strategy. You may be seeking participants with specific knowledge of your chosen topic, or those belonging to a particular category of people, such as parent, teacher, early years practitioner. Despite a recurring emphasis on the pursuit of objectivity and neutrality, participants in social research are frequently selected for their subjective knowledge, experience and membership of a particular category applicable to the research (Howarth 2002). Such memberships not only inform the data but provide a legitimacy to speak with authority on the topic (Baker 2003). It is this legitimate, authoritative knowledge, emanating from within category memberships that we, as researchers, seek. For example, the data from teachers, social workers or indeed children needs to be representative of that category. As researchers, we need/expect our participants to speak as members of the category we have positioned them in. However, when researching narratives of belonging with adopted children, Sarah became aware that her membership placement of children in what she considered to be the most significant category, that of adopted child, was often rejected by the children themselves. Her participants often identified other categories for themselves, such as a good friend; a member of the drama club; a school pupil, or simply, 'more than just adopted'. It was only through a reflexive process that Sarah began to recognize the ways in which the children resisted being exclusively placed in the category of adoption, the category she had situated them in and expected them to speak from. As discussed, the legitimacy afforded us as members of certain groups entitles us to hold specific knowledge associated with these categories and to speak about them with authority. As researchers we need to recognize that the categories we belong to shape how we interpret our data. Ristock and Pennell (1996: 66) claim that researchers should start their analyses from the personal and indicate the ways in which their locations and identities inform and shape the research process.

We hope that the examples we have given so far in this chapter have highlighted some of the ways in which our own positionalities, identities and category memberships have influenced reflexive considerations of our own research projects and the data produced. The next activity, 4.8, provides you with the opportunity to consider such aspects within your own research.

> **ACTIVITY 4.8**
> As a reflexive activity, consider the ways in which your category memberships shape your research interests.
> - Which category memberships do you perceive you have in common with your research participants?
> - Consider how your connections, positions and categories might influence your research decisions; the questions you ask, and your interpretations and analysis of the data you collect.
> - Reflect on how your participants are responding to you in your data collections. Do they talk to you as someone 'in the know'; a fellow professional; a fellow female researcher; a fellow parent; a fellow student? In other words, have they placed you in a same category as they are and do their responses reflect this implied membership?

As activity 4.8 may have revealed, category membership can position the researcher as an insider along with the participant (Taylor 2011). Such positioning offers an entitlement to speak with authenticity and authority on a particular topic. From the researcher's perspective, a participant's 'persuasiveness' can depend on the category membership the researcher has placed the participant in (Wenzel 2000: 158). Perceptions of entitlement are dependent upon where the participants and researcher have positioned themselves and have been positioned by each other. Lerner (1980) argues that such entitlements relate to who people think they are and how this category is positioned in the wider social context. People who are perceived as being similar are thus treated in a similar way (Perelman 1963).

It is, however, rather too simplistic to identify category memberships and assumed entitlements, such as gender, sexuality and class, and infer understanding, commonality or shared values. Howarth (2002: 23) contends assumptions that 'common social identification produce shared knowledge and experiences' is both patronizing and essentialistic'. However, we do still use these memberships and entitlements throughout the research process. Nevertheless, in qualitative research such groups can challenge the assumed attributes associated with negative category membership (Hacking 1986). Groups within a disempowered category, such as children or other marginalized groups, can use the qualitative turn in social research to challenge the characteristics they are assumed to hold. Clearly, our categorical memberships and entitlements as researchers, and those of our participants, play a significant role throughout research. Public acknowledgement of joint category membership between you and your participants can sometimes lead to what might be assumed to be dangerous territory. Based on this membership you might be asked by your participants to share your personal experiences and perceptions of the topic. The potential for this self-disclosure is explored next.

## Self-Disclosure

Dunbar, Rodriques and Parker (2002) contend that self-disclosure in research happens when a connection takes place between the researcher and the researched. In a similar way to category entitlement, the concept of self-disclosure is commonly neglected in social research discussions (Abell et al 2006). However, de Laine (1997) argues that qualitative research methods, by their very nature, invite disclosure. Concerns surrounding objectivity, validity and impartiality of the data may deter researchers from identifying when, or if, they have provided personal information about themselves in interviews or focus groups. A fear of 'contamination' in conventional research can inhibit such social interaction (Dunbar, Rodriques and Parker 2002: 138). Holstein and Gubrium (1995: 13) remind interviewers that they are commonly expected to keep their 'selves' separate from the interview process. As a result, research discussions can become sanitized, where self-disclosure and any connections between respondents and researchers are ignored. Thus, the potential for rich complexity in the analysis and discussion that self-disclosures can bring become unavailable. Like category entitlement, self-disclosure is most usually found within feminist methodological approaches where social interaction and research-based relationships are acknowledged and reflexively explored.

To actively self-disclose has been referred to as 'creative interviewing' where common but not necessarily comfortable ground can be established between participant and researcher (Dunbar, Rodriques and Parker 2002). As such, self-disclosure can be part of establishing or building relationships of trust with participants. Abell et al (2006: 224) argue that interviewers build category membership through self-disclosure to develop a rapport with participants, or to identify a difference with them. Activity 4.9 may help you to highlight certain instances where you have used self-disclosure in your conversations with participants.

### ACTIVITY 4.9
Considering your own data collection sessions, think about the ways in which you may have put your respondents at ease during interviews or focus groups.
- Did you share any information about yourself?
- At what points in your data collection process did you do this and why? For example, was it to welcome your participants, put them at their ease, establish a rapport or establish a common ground?

Reinharz (1997) has argued that within social research, the researcher should be recognized and utilized as an instrument, with tools such as personal experiences, identity characteristics or category memberships that can be applied within participatory methods. It is argued that when participants have a sense of being understood by someone who has, or has had, similar life experiences, trust can emerge (Oakley 1981). From a feminist stance, such investment into the relationship with participants, where their personal identity is shared, can provide greater insight into the research topic. Furthermore, the respondents may choose to share more information in response to the interviewer disclosing aspects of themselves (Oakley 1981). Though complex, data collection methods that involve reciprocity and rapport are increasingly seen as legitimate sources of data (Riessman 1994). Indeed, Jordan (2006) argues that obtaining rich, textured and situated knowledge about the lives of participants requires a certain amount of self-disclosure on the part of the researcher. It is argued that using self-disclosure can address and offset unequal relationships within the research process (Abell et al 2006: 221) and can even serve to empower participants (Eder and Fingerson 2003).

For example, when Sarah was researching with intercountry adopted children, she arrived at the house of a participant, Kate, who had changed her mind about taking part. Whilst Sarah was reassuring her that it was fine to say no, her mother was trying to persuade her to cooperate. Kate therefore found herself positioned between two opposing adults. Under such circumstances, she asked Sarah, 'why do you want to know about me being adopted'? Sarah disclosed that she wanted to learn about Kate's experiences of being adopted because Sarah had a much younger daughter who was also adopted from China. This prompted a further question from Kate relating to which province in China Sarah's daughter was from. It became apparent that both Sarah's daughter and Kate were from the same province. It was this disclosure that prompted Kate to take part. The interaction also established a shared category membership, and this bestowed an entitlement on Sarah to know and understand the knowledge that Kate chose to share.

# Limitations of Self-Disclosure

Whilst much of our discussion thus far has focused on the function of self-disclosure as a bringer of benefits to both participants and researchers, other perspectives are available. We have already observed how debates that value objectivity and neutrality position self-disclosure as a contaminant to the research encounter and the data produced. Similarly, rather than generate the trust, reciprocity and closeness we might expect, self-disclosure can emphasize differences between researcher and participants (Abell et al 2006). Such disparities can create obstacles to the establishment of further connections and relationship quality, and ultimately 'have the effect of positively suppressing further talk' (Abell et al 2006: 241). Self-disclosure can sometimes reveal the different category memberships of the researcher and researched rather than their joint memberships. One of the advantages of both researcher and participant being in the same category is that it encourages conversations and connection; however, if disclosure reveals difference, this can reduce or impede that conversation.

Dutton, Deanne and Bullen (2022: 129), for example, examined issues of self-disclosure on the part of the researcher during mentoring sessions with young people, noting 'a complex context for disclosure', in which 'an imbalanced power dynamic' was clear. Such hierarchical situations, they contend, illustrate how the authority and responsibility of adult mentors (and here we ask you to consider adult researchers) may lead to a reluctance to disclose on the part of participants. The act of self-disclosure is to encourage participants to share their experiences, yet as Dutton, Deanne and Bullen (2022) and Abell et al (2006) contend it can be counterproductive and reduce interactions. Furthermore, Dutton, Deanne and Bullen (2022: 129) raise additional issues, suggesting that thoughtful discretion and careful decisions need to be made by adults, in relation to the child's ability to deal with the 'emotional burden of disclosure', particularly in the case of sensitive topics. The topic, the context for disclosure, and who you are disclosing to become very important points to consider. Therefore, even if a specific disclosure is beneficial to your research, you must question if it is in the interests of your participant. Whether or not to self-disclose can easily become an ethical dilemma.

Furthermore, Hart and Crawford-Wright (1999) argue that self-disclosure can be perceived as exploitative of participants. To avert this, Liamputtong (2007: 74) agrees that researchers should think carefully about their research, its context, the amount of disclosure necessary and subsequently adopt a strategy where neither party feels 'constrained or embarrassed'. Therefore, not only do you need to consider your own position within the remit of self-disclosure as an adult researcher but your responsibilities towards children and young people. Activity 4.10 encourages you to think about how you would respond when invited to self-disclose during an interview.

### ACTIVITY 4.10
How would you respond if you were researching children's perceptions of family life, and a child asks about your own family life.
- Would you close the conversation?
- Would you deflect the conversation by saying I'm here to learn about your family?
- Would you provide a minimum of information?
- Would you share your own experience of family life?

There isn't necessarily right or wrong answers to activity 4.10. Aspects which shape how you respond may include consideration of who is asking, the research context and whether disclosing is beneficial to all concerned. These are complex and ethical decisions to make in the moment but the discussions around them are highly relevant to your dissertation.

Despite the above points the more usual discussions around self-disclosure relate to safeguarding. For instance, how should the researcher respond to disclosures that may occur during research when a child or group of children, purposefully or inadvertently, disclose something that concerns you – the central theme being how disclosures are managed. At the very start of your dissertation, when obtaining consent from children, your documentation will have highlighted the anonymous and confidential nature of your discussions. However, this will have contained one caveat, that is, if children share something that worries you, then you will have to disclose this to members of staff. If your research context is a school or nursery, you will follow the settings safeguarding protocols and pass your concerns onto the safeguarding teams. If your research is taking place within an organization such as the scouting movement, they will also have a safeguarding lead. Therefore, before carrying out your research it is worthwhile to familiarize yourself with safeguarding protocols within that setting. Activity 4.11 should help you with this.

---

**ACTIVITY 4.11**

Your research project takes place in a school where you are working as a part-time learning support assistant. The children involved are in year 6.

Whilst carrying out your research a child mentions to you that they are being bullied by others in their class.

- What will you do?

---

## Applying Key Concepts to Your Dissertation

Greenbank (2003: 798) contends that 'the inclusion of reflective accounts and the acknowledgement that ... research cannot be value free should be included in all forms of research'. In accordance with this claim, we now identify ways in which you can include the concepts discussed earlier in this chapter (subjectivity, reflexivity, category memberships and entitlements, positionality, self-disclosure) in your research project.

Starting at the beginning, your introduction can be a useful place to present salient aspects of yourself to the reader that illustrate and inform your interests in, and relationships with, your topic. Moving on, the methodology section equally offers opportunities for the utilization of research concepts. For example, you could outline the relevance of subjectivity and reflexivity to your research approach and knowledge construction. Furthermore, recognition of specific categories and positionalities to which you belong or identify with can act as analytical tools when exploring your data. The exploration and analysis of such concepts within and throughout your dissertation will better demonstrate your critical knowledge and understanding of your role within the research.

Acting as the summative section of your dissertation, a critical self-review becomes a valuable opportunity to exhibit highly reflexive consideration of your research journey. By this we do not mean reflecting on what you did and when during your research project, and how you might do it differently another time. Rather, we ask you to evaluate pertinent aspects of your dissertation by viewing them through the lens/es of the concepts provided here. For example, you could include your perceptions of how differing positions that you hold, or roles that you play, may have influenced your interpretation and analysis of your data. If you self-disclosed during your fieldwork or were asked to by participants, you could examine your decisions and their implications, in more detail. Furthermore, this section is very often written in the first person and can pick up aspects of your positionality outlined in your introduction as being relevant to how you conducted and produced your research. In this way these concepts become coherent, recurring themes throughout the whole of your dissertation. The research-based conversations that such deliberations bring can better demonstrate your critical knowledge of the relationship between seemingly remote concepts and the closeness of self, and ultimately elevate your dissertation.

# Conclusion

In conclusion, this chapter has explored some complex, and yet, essential concepts, which you can now aspire to utilize and discuss within your dissertation. Such concepts encourage and enable you and your readers to recognize, and positively position, you/yourself/selves throughout the entirety of your work. Indeed, we have outlined how you might explicitly acknowledge this involvement of self, and articulate its consequences, in the research relationships that you build. The incorporation of such ideas, and their interrogation, demonstrates a deeper perceptiveness of the involvement of self in the research process and adds the 'thick description' (Geertz 1973) that qualitative researchers seek.

Initially, notions of subjectivity, reflexivity, positionality and so on may have appeared inaccessible, remote and detached from yourself. However, we now encourage you to welcome these ideas, consider them as useful research tools and through them allow you and your presence to become visible in your research.

# 5

# Worrying That 'I've Got No Data'

## Introduction

Carrying out research with children is often fun and illuminating but seldom straightforward. We attest that children who participate in research might not always be so easily biddable as their adult counterparts. Children often present us with their own agendas in the research process, their own timescales and their own emphases, some or even many of which, may not be ours. For these reasons and many others, we can confidently assert that research with children is challenging, messy and complex, and thus the data produced by child-led research can, at first, appear tangled and ambiguous, leading us to question, what, if any, relevant data do we have.

In relation to this dilemma, a recurrent theme in our dissertation supervision has been to support students who return from their fieldwork and anxiously pronounce 'I've got no data'. Suddenly, all the excitement and anticipation of carrying out the research dissipates, only to be replaced by reduced confidence and a looming sense of failure. Despite all reassurances made throughout the project that a student dissertation is about demonstrating a critical understanding of the research process itself, the student's attention has often been elsewhere, that is, on what they find. Therefore, the assumption of 'no data' can be devastating. If this is currently your situation, we hope this chapter, and further discussions with your supervisor, will help you recognize that you do have data, even if it's not quite what you expected to find.

We begin this chapter by discussing the plans you need to make, and put in place, prior to collecting your data, and some of the dilemmas that can arise during data collection. Following this we ask you to overcome your perceived lack of findings by recognizing what you have gathered from your participants as your data. We discuss how you might present data in a rich and contextualized format, which resists being reductive. Subsequently, your analysis should develop key topics and arguments that are predominantly led by the voices of your participants and supported by the key texts identified in your literature review. However, before we embroil ourselves in the mysteries of analysing our data, we must first set out a plan of how to collect it.

# Steps in Data Collection

## Planning Your Data Collection

Collecting data can be challenging and requires thoughtful consideration of methods and context. Gallacher and Gallagher (2008: 513) suggest that 'what matters is not so much the methods used, but the ways and the spirit in which they are used: the methodological attitude taken'. We consider this to be an important point and reiterate the centrality of sincerity and care in our research encounters. Respecting participants, as discussed in previous chapters, underpins the building of relationships and trust, which enable children to participate, and potentially, have their voices heard. Listening to these voices and representing them thoughtfully and honestly are the foundations on which your research needs to be built. Back (2007) refers to this in his book *The Art of Listening* and considers ways in which we might listen more carefully. As a sociologist Back contends that the discipline should provide space for the things that cannot be said, provide respect for the uncelebrated, champion alternative stories, produce critical and open-minded accounts, and have a desire to listen and take the people we listen to as seriously as ourselves. Surely a pertinent aspiration for students and researchers of childhood.

Collecting data does not happen by chance and requires a solid plan. We provide activity 5.1 for your consideration, and in association with your own planning. The listed items are not exhaustive in their remit; however, they are intended to help you recognize the importance of planning and its relationship to data collection success.

---

## ACTIVITY 5.1
Points to consider and check as you prepare to collect data.
- Ensure you have access to a setting.
- Confirm permissions from gatekeepers. (For example, alongside the headteacher or setting lead, make sure that other teachers are also aware, and willing, for you to conduct your data collection in their classroom.)
- Verify consent from gatekeepers and participants. Affirm and reaffirm as necessary.
- Commit to agreed timeframe arrangements with the setting. (This may require some negotiation, so as not to be intrusive to the teaching agenda or where children might lose cherished playtime.)
- Check the activity fits into the time and location you have been given. (Some possible pitfalls we have experienced with students include the following two examples: Your activity is a creative one, potentially taking up to an hour to complete, and you have only been given thirty minutes with the children. Or similarly, you are planning a noisy activity and have been given the library in which to do it.) In both cases planning and communication beforehand could have averted such issues.

- Check you have prepared all the materials required for your activity and have them in sufficient quantities.
- Familiarize your participants with any equipment you will be asking them to use. This may require you to factor in additional time, for example, using disposable cameras.
- Organize a recording device and take some extra time to introduce and explain its purpose to the children. Your participants may enjoy listening to their voices being played back to them, but this could become of greater interest than your topic. Therefore, consider the possibility of requesting a short session prior to the actual data collection in which you could introduce the children to new equipment and resources.
- Before starting check that your participants understand the activity and, in the light of ongoing consent with children, remain happy to take part.

Despite the best plans, we have, over the years, had multiple examples of students returning from their data collections with stories of their perceived failure to get the data they expected from the children. For example, we had a dissertation student who wanted to explore children's perceptions of their classroom environment. The student aimed to do this by gathering photographs, taken by the children on disposable cameras, followed by conversations with the children to contextualize their perspectives of the images. However, this focus was initially lost, as the children, excited by what was new technology to them, enthusiastically chose to take random pictures, sometimes of friends, rather than those more closely related to the research topic. This was followed by multiple questions from the children concerning the immediate whereabouts of the images, this from a generation of children used to digital cameras. Luckily the student was able to negotiate an extended period of data collection, which allowed the children to relax into the activity more fully and generate the looked-for data. Now consider activity 5.2.

> **ACTIVITY 5.2**
> Using the previously outlined scenario involving digital cameras.
> - How would you plan to avoid a similar situation?

In response to activity 5.2 you may have suggested setting up an activity with the children, sometime prior to the data collection, where you introduce the cameras and allow the children to take pictures. Setting up an information and familiarization session is not time wasted, rather it provides you with information about the process of doing research with children and allows your data collection to focus on your research topic more easily. Subsequently, writing about this session can enhance your methodological and reflexive discussions. However, negotiating an extra session can be challenging within the remit of the school day and may call for further permissions. Therefore, it is often more straightforward to allocate extra time at the start and end of your actual data collection session. The key here is to be prepared and plan, in the likely event of children being diverted. However, even with the best planning, data collection may not always go as expected or anticipated but this may not be the disaster you imagined.

## Collecting Your Data

Having planned your data, you can now embark upon collection, this can be both exciting and anxiety inducing, not least because despite extensive planning things do not always go the way you intend. For example, we supervised a student whose research focus was on children's involvement in their communities. This student had planned for focus groups and drawing activities, and had an agreed time set aside when the children and the classroom were available to her. All permissions were in place and the equipment needed was ready. However, it just so happened that on her data collection day it snowed heavily. Not only did some of the children not make it to school but those that did only wanted to talk about snow. A distraught student returned to her dissertation supervision session with a collection of beautiful snow drawings and digital recordings of snow stories. The time constraints of her dissertation, and equally of the school timetable, meant this was her only opportunity to collect data. Think about what you might do if faced with such circumstances.

In response to the above situation, rather than a discussion and analysis of children's communitarianism, we instead encouraged the student to write a critical discussion on the realities and challenges of doing research with children. The snow data was used as evidence of how children can, and do, exert the agency enshrined in the philosophy of child-centred methodologies. As supervisors, we reiterated that it is the critical knowledge and understanding of research that must be demonstrated in a dissertation, rather than simply or only, what you find. Sometimes, the best research discussions emerge when something unexpected happens in the field (see Coombs and Richards 2023).

Clearly collecting data involves being flexible and adaptive to changing circumstances. For example, another of our students had to manage the repercussions on her research after the sudden and unexpected death of the headteacher. This person was the gatekeeper for her research, and with whom she had negotiated permissions and access for her dissertation project. Perhaps understandably, the interim headteacher withdrew permission on the basis that the school was trying to readjust after such difficult circumstances. We tried to reassure the student to be patient and allow the setting, and its children, time to settle. In the meantime, we worked with the student to simplify her activity and its aim, so that if she was eventually allowed to conduct her data collection it would fit more readily into the school day and be less intrusive to the school community. Fortunately, this strategy was successful. We were able to encourage the student to think and write reflexively about the often underexplored relational skills required by researchers during their fieldwork. Concepts such as flexibility, understanding, patience and recognition of a trauma-informed approach, along with communication and the importance of an ethic of care, are all examples of how you can explore research relationships in your dissertation.

The examples above help us to recognize the diverse and everyday challenges that researchers face when they embark on their research projects. Both experienced and inexperienced researchers of childhood need to be adaptable to changing circumstances, some of which, as we have seen, can be testing and beyond our control. Such events can derail us, make us throw up our hands in despair and/or bury our heads in the sand but there is almost always a way around and through such situations. Here, the importance of working with your supervisor cannot be emphasized enough. Your relationship is crucial, and you must bring any difficulties, barriers and issues to your supervisor in a timely manner, so you can work together to find solutions. What might, at first, seem insurmountable problems may simply require small changes or adjustments to your research activities, so they fit more readily into the requirements of the setting and its children.

Although research with children calls for the detailed planning illustrated in this chapter, it also requires its researchers to be pragmatic, agile and creative in the moment. Research with children is not always predictable, and ad hoc or impromptu decisions are sometimes required to achieve practical and ethical solutions to the everyday issues we might experience. Using some examples previously highlighted in this volume, review activity 5.3 and ask yourself, what would you do in these situations. It is often unexpected events that invite us to question and re-question the responses we made at the time. It is unlikely that we all respond in the same way but through acknowledging our reactions and sharing them with others we can help to produce more critically reflexive and honest accounts of our fieldwork (see Richards and Coombs 2023).

> **ACTIVITY 5.3**
>
> Explore the following examples confronted by students and ourselves during fieldwork. Ask yourself, what would you do in these situations?
> - A child who had given consent to take part in a research project makes it clear that they want to withdraw during the data collection session. Considering ongoing consent with children, the student agrees, and the child is returned safely to their classroom. The teacher then brings the child back saying to the student researcher that the child needs to remain and continue the activity. How would you respond?
> - A student who was a teaching assistant in the setting is carrying out a memory game with a group of children as part of her research. A teacher walks in and starts engaging the student in conversation about a lesson taking place later. How would you respond?
> - Despite child and parental permissions being giving to planned research activities the teacher refuses to let a child take part, pointing to their poor behaviour on the previous day. How would you respond?

If something insurmountable happens that prevents you from collecting your data with participants, do not despair. Whilst this can be initially stressful and worrying, it can also lead you to alternative, but equally exciting ways, to conduct your research. For example, your supervisor might suggest that you explore your chosen subject through a discourse analysis using newspaper articles that cover the topic, or via an exploration of children's picture books, teenage fiction or indeed relevant films. All these are fascinating and legitimate ways to collect data. We have supervised students who have explored representations of the family through a selection of children's story books, depictions of gender stereotypes in the Mr Men and Little Miss series of books, portrayals of girlhoods in children's magazines, and serious case reviews and headline hitting stories of child refugees through newspaper reports. Equally, examining your topic by means of theoretical perspectives, policies or differing models, such as models of health and/or disability, are also extremely productive and stimulating alternatives to research with child participants. For example, students have investigated a variety of topics by adopting theoretical perspectives such as social constructionism and/or developmentalism, they have looked at the worlds of children with disabilities through contrasting medical and social models, and they have interrogated education, welfare and health policies in relation to children and families. These alternative ways of collecting data, by means of information found in the media, online, in literature, and a myriad of other places, have provided thoughtful and considered insights into aspects of childhood. Such approaches have often been used to explore sensitive topics that would be difficult to investigate as a novice researcher with children, and in so doing have produced some thought provoking and critically informed dissertations.

Notwithstanding some of the concerns illustrated above, data collection is often a student's favourite aspect of their dissertation. After all your planning you will be excited to carry out your research, as you begin to realize your research aims, utilize the methods and methodologies you have thought about for so long, and work with your young participants. While this is an exciting time it can also understandably generate some anxiety as students can worry about their competency to carry out research having perhaps never done it before. You may be concerned about who, if any, will arrive to carry out the activity, and here we can reassure you by saying that if only one or two children arrive, then carry on. Students can often express anxiety about what might happen during the session, what children might say, or perhaps more specifically, not say, and therefore as the researcher will you manage to capture any relevant data at all. Hopefully our content has reassured you, demonstrating that there are always solutions, and such dilemmas are experienced by every researcher.

## Recognizing Your Data

Successfully completing your fieldwork is a massive step in the progress of your dissertation and you should congratulate yourself on reaching this point. Yet, it is often at this moment, as students begin to listen to their recordings, transcribe children's conversations and appraise the outcomes of various activities that assertions of 'having no data', in fact having 'nothing at all', become prevalent. However, when asked to bring this 'nothingness' to supervision, it often becomes clear that lovely data does indeed exist, even if it is not quite what was expected. Arguably, as researchers, we are so invested in our topic, the methods we will use, the questions we will ask, the theories we will employ and the literature we will interrogate, and, even if we don't admit it, what we think we will find, that we cannot initially see the wood for the trees. However, we have found that by standing back a little and bringing your data into a supervision session, that you can begin to see your findings in a different light. The very act of discussing your transcripts with your supervisor can help. These discussions can help you recognize key features in your data, which may not have been initially apparent. These features can help you identify and explore alternative, and perhaps unexpected, themes. Even if you think you have no usable data, with time and careful consideration you will find that you have. This data may not be what you expected to find, nevertheless it is the data provided by your participants through the questions you asked. Not getting the data you thought can lead you to a critical exploration of whether you asked appropriate questions. This reflexive activity is, in itself, a useful discussion point in your dissertation, particularly in sections such as the self-critical review.

Even with appropriate questions the data received can be unexpected. For example, we remember a student who was exploring children's perspectives of healthy eating through conversations and drawings. One of her participants produced a drawing of a large chocolate cream cake. The student's first assumption was that the child had not understood what was being asked of them. Subsequently, she became concerned that this data was not relevant to her dissertation as it represented what she assumed was the antithesis of healthy eating. However, the child went on to explain that large chocolate cream cakes make her happy, that being happy is a good thing, and therefore healthy. So, having first assumed this data was unusable the student ultimately realized the importance of listening to children's explanations and how their views do not necessarily follow key doctrines that often inform our practice. Therefore, rather than no data, this example developed into a key theme within her analysis and discussions.

Such examples call us to interrogate our own powerful adult positions in our research, to analyse our preconceived ideas, and to ask if we are genuinely interested in children's perspectives or just looking for children to corroborate our adult views of the world.

## Managing Unexpected Data

Receiving cream cakes when you were expecting broccoli reminds us that children, as agentic actors, can take us on unexpected journeys in their responses to our questions. As researchers, how we respond to this unexpected data can be a concern, particularly in how we reply to the participant in the moment, what actions we should take and the ramifications for our research. Children can say unanticipated things. Such unexpected data, offered within a focus group for example, can easily divert the attention of children, and quickly take the conversation in a different direction. On occasion, as in some research that we ourselves conducted, such a diversion not only led the conversation off topic but also inadvertently strayed into a sensitive theme. For this research, we collected stories from young children aged around five years old, whose playground was originally part of a graveyard. During this activity, religious beliefs came to the fore. In explaining the purpose of gravestones, one child declared that there were bones underneath them, and that this was not problematic because the dead do not come back to life. Another child then declared that 'Jesus did'. As researchers we had to manage a group of children from diverse backgrounds and religions. On the one hand, we needed to uphold the child's belief in their claim, whilst not appearing to affirm this belief over others that might be present. We remained silent and allowed the conversation to naturally develop into a broader theme about various activities of the dead.

Here, stories of zombies, vampires and angels were shared. The exuberance of children offering their thoughts about the occupants of gravestones in their play area reduced the possibility of further questions concerning the claim of the return of Jesus. Attempting to remain neutral through silence was therefore perhaps the most appropriate action on our part as it gave equal credence to all perspectives shared that day.

As researchers we can often carry unacknowledged assumptions about the data we may collect into our fieldwork. One way to recognize this is if we are surprised or even disconcerted by the responses of our participants. For example, one of our students was collecting data around the topic of children's perceptions of superheroes. One child drew an image of their mother, and the student, in supervision, declared this to be 'unusable'. She felt the child had not understood the task at hand. As supervisors, we addressed this perspective by asking what the child had said about their drawing. The student disclosed that the child's reply had been 'my Mum is my superhero'. We asked the student to reflect on what she had assumed she would find. We then encouraged her to analyse this example as part of her data rather than discard it for the more obvious data examples of Batman, Spiderman and Catwoman. We were emphatic that this was amazing data, although perhaps, not what she originally assumed she would find. Furthermore, we encouraged this student to be reflexive in her dissertation about the assumptions she held concerning what the children would say.

Predetermined expectations of your data, especially if you unearth surprising finds, can create anxiety. Ideally therefore, you should carry out activity 5.4 before commencing your data collection as it can help you realize how much of yourself you are bringing into the field. Fixed assumptions can prevent you from recognizing the rich data you may have, that is, cream cake as healthy food and Mother as superhero. If our findings do not fall in line with our adult assumptions, we must ask ourselves if we are ready to hear what children have to say or merely wish to maintain the adult status quo. Are we ready to prioritize what we have found over what we thought we might find.

> **ACTIVITY 5.4**
> Interrogating your assumptions.
> - What assumption did/do you have about your own topic?
> - What did/do you think children might say about your topic?
> - How are your assumptions shaping your expectations of your data?

What children say cannot only surprise us but can also conflict with our beliefs and world views. In Montgomery's (2007) research with child prostitutes in Thailand the children were emphatic about their agentic choice to engage in these activities for the benefits of their families. Despite Montgomery's desire to listen and hear the voices of these children she felt unable to accept their version of these activities being anything other than abuse. Respecting the childrens agency and expertise in their own worlds therefore became challenging for her. This ultimately led her to act on her beliefs and take one participant to hospital despite her previous assurances to the community and her participants that such measures would not be taken. This action ultimately undermined her relationships with this community, and she writes reflexively about the methodological and ethical dilemmas that she encountered (Montgomery 2023).

Whilst Montgomery's research is an extreme example, children can nevertheless disclose unanticipated information during data collection that necessitates actions on the part of the researcher. Activity 5.5 can help you to consider what you might do under such circumstances.

> **ACTIVITY 5.5**
> You are in a school setting collecting data about wearing school uniform. You are using focus groups as a method and have four children sitting with you at a table whilst drawing and talking. One child quietly shares with you that they fear certain children in their class. When questioned further by the researcher it becomes clear that this is an example of bullying.
> - How should you respond?

Your response to activity 5.5 must involve informing the safeguarding officers within the school or setting, who can then enact the school's safeguarding policy. However, in the moment of the disclosure it is important to support the child and explain how you will need to respond as previously outlined in the information letters to your participants. As part of your ongoing verbal discussions with your participants you should reiterate the actions you will take if a disclosure is made.

As a researcher what can be equally anxiety inducing in data collection is children who stay silent. With all the emphasis on children's voices it is often easy to neglect the reality that children can not only choose to speak but can also choose to stay silent. As dissertation supervisors we have often experienced students who return from their fieldwork with what they consider to be a lack of data. Students have worriedly expressed, that individual children remained silent throughout their participatory methods. This again was often construed, on the student's part, as having no data. In contrast to this perspective, we encouraged students to consider silence as the counterpoint to voice. We argue that both decisions are equally agentic, and therefore should be recognized as meaningful data. Rather than be tempted to interpret these silences using our own voice, we should instead recognize that silence can provide an opportunity to contextualize the environment in which a particular child remained silent or indeed chose to speak.

Activity 5.6 encourages you to consider the circumstances under which a child may choose to remain silent, what their silences may mean and your responsibilities as the researcher. Such deliberations should help you to contextualize the circumstances and environments in which we, as researchers, ask children to speak.

> **ACTIVITY 5.6**
> You are collecting data with a small group of children in a school setting and one child remains silent.
> Consider the possible reasons for, and implications of, their silence.
> - Has this child chosen to withdraw? If so, what are your responsibilities here?
> - Do you know if the child is friends with the other children in the group? Could this friendship or lack of friendship be related to this child's silence?
> - If your activity is taking place in a school, have you assumed that this is a safe space for this child?
> - Have you established sufficient rapport with this child, thus enabling them to contribute?
> - Are you sure the child has relevant experiences related to the topic at hand, for example are you asking a child who has packed lunches to discuss school dinners?

In our research encounters, when a child remains silent or offers unexpected responses, it is easy to assume that we have no meaningful data. However, here we need to look creatively at what we do have and respond with an open mind. Silences can be meaningful. Unexpected data can be treasures, which can take us in new and unanticipated directions. As researchers, we need to weave these features into our dissertations. Perhaps it is helpful to think of ourselves as bricoleurs, quilt makers (Denzin and Lincoln 2008), who sew or weave our analysis together to create a rich and elaborate montage. As Denzin and Lincoln state (2008: 7 and 8), 'the quilter stiches, edits, and puts slices of reality together', the result being 'a complex, quilt-like bricolage, a reflexive collage or montage – a set of fluid, interconnected images and representations'. As qualitative researchers ourselves we chose an image of a quilt as a symbol for the Children and Childhoods Conference that runs biennially at the University of Suffolk. Its richness, jewel-like refractive qualities and colourfulness epitomized for us the complexities and intricacies of being qualitative researchers with children.

## The Cutting Room Floor

Having discussed ways to recognize your data, another aspect of managing this can mean making some hard decisions about what to include and exclude in your final dissertation. We therefore now explore how to make such choices and highlight the availability to do so throughout your dissertation.

We find ourselves attached to our data because we remember the contexts and circumstances in which it was produced, and indeed the children who created it. Consequently, it can be hard to leave any out. However, we know it is not feasible to include every conversation and every quote into our discussions. We must recognize when to stop, or must we? Activity 5.7 helps you think about how and where you might include some of your much-loved data that has, so far, ended up on the cutting room floor.

---

**ACTIVITY 5.7**

You have lots of data left over from your research that did not quite make it into your final discussions and arguments. Nevertheless, you would still like to incorporate some of it if you can.
- Consider where you might include it beyond your discussion and findings section.

---

Your engagement with activity 5.7 has perhaps revealed to you how you might creatively incorporate pieces of data into other aspects of your dissertation. To begin, you might usefully incorporate a quote from one of your participants into your title. For example, as part of Sarah's PhD title she used the following quote *'We're ok with death'*. Sarah felt this comment, made by one of her participants, succinctly described all that the children had been telling her, and thus the title became, '*We're ok with death*': *Young people discuss the end of life*. In a similar way, quotes can also be used as chapter headings or act as useful subheadings, especially when presenting data that illustrates key themes in your findings. Notwithstanding these areas, data may also be usefully deployed throughout your dissertation to highlight key methodological, ethical or reflexive points, or indeed concluding remarks. The skill is to utilize what you can by selecting and including the pieces of data that have the most impact and contribute insights into your key arguments. Similarly, copies of children's drawings, photographs or other creative materials, which have not been used in your analysis or discussions, can provide colourful intersections between dissertation chapters and content. Using data in this way helps to bring children's voices and contributions to the forefront of your dissertation, which is where they should be, rather than discarded and left on the cutting room floor.

# Conclusion

In conclusion, our intentions for this chapter were to encourage students, anxious about their lack of data or its content, to feel more confident about its application to their topic and the development of their dissertation. Therefore, this chapter was written as a response to so many of our students, who immediately after data collection, worriedly suggested that they had no relevant data. In our discussions above, we have focused on planning for successful data collection, the act of collecting the data as well as how to recognize the data that we have. Following this we also explored how to respond to unexpected data including disclosures and silences. Finally, we encouraged the use of data to populate not only the findings and discussion chapter but also within ethical, methodological and reflexive discussions and throughout the dissertation, as titles, chapter headings, subheadings and concluding remarks.

# 6

# Putting 'I' into Research with Children

## Introduction

The aim of this final chapter is to assist you in finding your own narrative voice within and throughout your research. We hope to equip you with the instruments and agency to firmly acknowledge your presence in your study, and recognize the multiple ways in which you, as a unique individual, are undeniably 'in' your research. Some of the most satisfying dissertations to read are those where the voice of the student researcher is distinct and reflexively acknowledged.

Conducting and writing research has often been an endeavour where the writer attempts to ensure their absence from the written page. Hyland (2001: 207) refers to this as 'a modest, self-effacing task which involves authors eradicating themselves from their texts to gain acceptance for their work'. In other words, and across many disciplines, part of the convention of academic writing has been to present an objective account, where the personality and positionality of the author do not intrude. Nevertheless, as we will explore later in this chapter, writers from within such conventions often utilize writing styles that may implicitly position them within their writing.

In contrast to the oblique inclusion described above, writers from a principally qualitative and participatory research approach more normatively recognize that their category memberships, positionality and existing research experiences can be privileged as sources of insight. Indeed, Jackson and Mazzei (2008) argue that these forms of writing, where there is a prevalence of the personal, are a valuable step away from the orthodox social sciences. However, at undergraduate and postgraduate levels of study, students can be reluctant to bring in, or may find themselves discouraged from, such inclusions. No matter how qualitative the methodology, restrictions often centre around the inclusion of the first-person pro-noun, thus producing 'a silent authorship' (Charmaz and Mitchel 1997: 193).

In contrast, the stance we take in this chapter is in accordance with Spivak (1976: lxxvii), whose eloquent perspective is that our writing is 'always already palimpsest'. Meaning that, who we are remains, despite any attempt to abstract or distance ourselves, and objectify our claims. To clarify, a palimpsest often refers to a written surface, which may have been partially erased and then reused, perhaps many times, and yet the original work remains relatively distinguishable. We agree with Spivak that no matter how hard we might try to eradicate ourselves from our own research projects, we cannot and, arguably, should not. We are present in our work and should openly acknowledge it. Perhaps a more contemporary analogy to the palimpsest would be a computer hard drive, where our data history lingers despite attempts at deletion.

This chapter initially outlines prevailing arguments for the exclusion of self in academic prose before building arguments for its inclusion. Each approach is illustrated by examples from published research. Here we also advance ideas about the ways in which you might acknowledge yourself in your own research discussions.

# Arguments against Using 'I' in Academic Writing

A casual glance through research textbooks highlights how specific disciplines take different approaches to the inclusion of the first-person pronoun. Traditionally, scientific and academic writing has been presented through the objective accounts of essentially anonymous and autonomous authors. Charmaz and Mitchel (1997: 193) argue that 'scholarly writers have long been admonished to work silently on the sidelines, to keep their voices out of the reports they produce, to emulate Victorian children: be seen (in the credits) but not heard (in the text)'. Additionally, Biber and Gray (2010: 2) maintain that 'the stereotypical view of professional academic writing is that it is grammatically complex, with elaborated structures'. Furthermore, they argue that such writing is 'decontextualised' and 'autonomous'. This complexity of writing style, and specifically the exclusion of 'self', has become synonymous with scientific and scholarly endeavour and is, as Hyland (2001: 208) claims, a 'hallowed concept for many'. Indeed, to further emphasize this point, Hyland (2001: 208) draws upon Einstein's (1934: 113) assertion that 'when a man is talking about scientific subjects, the little word "I" should play no part in his expositions'.

Notwithstanding such arguments, we contend that not only has the gender of researchers moved on from Einstein's statement but so too has the debate about the use of 'I' in academic writing. Whilst some disciplines, such as ethnography and feminist research, have embraced the presence of self and the inclusion of the first-person pronoun, it is evident that the convention of impersonal academic writing often remains resolute. Moreover, McCrostie (2008) contends that in English academia the emphasis is primarily on the topic and the evidence, rather than the presence of the writer or indeed the reader, both of whom remain marginalized. This assertion appears to remain true for English-speaking academics more broadly, perhaps due, in-part, to somewhat entrenched assumptions that impersonal writing has traditionally had greater claims to authoritative and valid knowledge. Such depersonalized prose provides the appearance of objectivity, which is argued to elicit greater credibility from the reader and implies that research outcomes would be the same regardless of who was conducting it (Hyland 2001). The exclusion of 'self' is therefore a tactic and/or convention that helps create an illusion of neutrality and elevates the impartiality of the author. In positioning findings and claims made as unbiased and factual, they become more readily acceptable to the reader. As Lachowicz (1981: 111) contends, the absence of 'self' accentuates objectivity and open-mindedness and highlights the 'common share of knowledge with the community'.

Lester (1993: 208) similarly argues that you should write your paper with a third-person voice that avoids 'I believe' or 'It is my opinion'. Using appropriate language and avoiding personal bias are a foundation of the positivist value that research should be essentially empirical, objective and value free. To achieve this aim, writing should be devoid of the presence or indication of the researcher. As a student, you will, no doubt, have been told that academic writing should be objective when expressing ideas and that you should avoid the inclusion of personal perspectives. Indeed, Plummer (2001: 181) emphasizes that 'most students are told *not* to use the first-person "I"' but rather instructed 'to write in a third person's voice, a neutral authority from outside the text'. Furthermore, he goes on to suggest that such 'authoritative modes of writing' are dominant within the social sciences and have been bestowed on us 'from on high by the men in black frocks and white coats'.

The multidisciplinary approach of childhood studies embraces diverse disciplines, such as psychology, sociology, social policy, history, anthropology and education, to name a few. Evidently, within this broad field a multitude of perspectives towards research are embraced, and subsequently the results of these different approaches are illuminating. However, the first-person pronoun is normatively absent in much research into childhood and with children. This is due, in part perhaps, to the historical reliance of childhood studies on psychology and developmentalism with their traditional pursuit of positivist approaches to research. Here, and in emerging welfare, education, wellbeing and social policy models there has been a perceived need for objective, generalizable knowledge, which make so-called, 'valid' and 'reliable' claims across large populations of children. Undoubtedly, this type of approach has also been compounded by assumptions regarding children's lack of agency and a historical disinterest in children's perspectives. The 'new' sociology of childhood and contemporary childhood studies have embraced a children's rights agenda. However, the field remains somewhat dominated by a desire for perceived objectivity, and unlike feminist approaches, childhood research has not yet entirely embraced first-person concepts such as positionality, reflexivity and first-person accounts. Clearly, childhood scholars are drawn from a variety of disciplines and, as such, bring conventions from their own specialisms to their research, teaching and dissertation supervision.

Consider activity 6.1 and the ways in which disciplines you have encountered throughout your degree may have influenced your writing.

### ACTIVITY 6.1
Reflect upon the various disciplines represented in the academic team who have taught you during your degree studies.
- In what ways might these different backgrounds have influenced the ways in which these academics write and research?
- In turn, how has this shaped your own research values and writing style?

Chang and Swales (1999: 164) researched students' perspectives on the use and avoidance of the first-person pronoun and contend that 'feelings and reactions can be both strong and unpredictable'. Therefore, in a group of thirty-seven graduate students, many felt uncomfortable utilizing the word I, suggesting that 'nobody likes to use it in a formal paper'. Indeed, Petch-Tyson (1998) argues that university students are rather invisible in their written work. Popular advice, it would seem, suggests that students should construct their arguments without reference to the first-person pronoun. This is certainly a stance often found in research guides and textbooks (Arnaudet and Barrett 1984). Cadman (1997: 8) argues that students can be uncertain about 'who they are expected to be' and are often unable to establish their own position in their writing. Conflicting advice in texts and from supervisors can compound these uncertainties. Yet, as previously suggested, conventions vary across disciplines. Hence, Yilmaz (2013) highlights the presence of a personal voice within certain research methodologies, together with a more engaging narrative style that can include the first-person pronoun. For example, 'I' is sometimes found within ethnographic research discussions, where it is accepted and even expected. In such cases it might feasibly even appear 'odd' if the first-person pronoun were not used.

Dissertation supervisors too will have expectations about which conventions you should follow, and therefore discussion about your narrative style and voice should form part of your supervision meetings. Begin by considering the particular discipline/s, which inform your research and remind yourself of the conventions associated with them. Talk to your supervisor but also first and foremost ask yourself, 'How do I want to be present in my research?' In our own doctoral research projects, we had little choice concerning this question. Our close relationship to our topics, and connections with the participants, required that we acknowledge our presence. As a result, and in contrast to previous research we had completed, we chose to be visible. However, reading through our aforementioned accounts we now recognize our presence in them, even in the absence of us using the word 'I'. Now we actively choose methodological approaches that acknowledge and celebrate the presence of the researcher's subjective positions.

We believe it is worth highlighting here the ways in which self-reference, even if unintentionally, emerges in supposedly impersonal scientific accounts. Indeed, somewhat counterintuitively, it is often explicitly used to enhance and increase the authority of the claims made. One common example occurs when a writer references their previous publications where similar and relevant arguments have already been presented. This self-reference is intended to strengthen the authoritative knowledge of the author in making arguments by suggesting that they are particularly entitled or knowledgeable about a topic. Sullivan (1996) and Hyland (2001) argue that such first-person reference activity is part of how academics demonstrate their identities within their respective disciplines as well as establish and strengthen their arguments in the field. Even when this occurs, authors may still claim a distanced objective perspective concerning the knowledge that has been generated. Yet, it does reveal the author to the reader, perhaps in unintended ways, regardless of the presence or absence of a first-person pronoun.

---

### ACTIVITY 6.2

Select an academic journal that you are familiar with and read through a few of the articles. Do not feel the need to engage in hours of literature searching, you could use the journals and articles you have already sourced for your own ongoing research.
- Highlight where and how often the authors self-reference earlier work.
- Identify how such referencing is used. Does it strengthen a claim or highlight/promote an existing position in a particular field?
- What do you as the reader learn about the researcher by these references and how does it make you think about the arguments they make?

---

If you feel that activity 6.2 has not sufficiently revealed to you the presence of researchers in their own writing, then try activity 6.3. This time, use your own work, taken from modules that you have studied across your degree course, to conduct the same activity. This should now help to highlight 'you' within your own papers.

> **ACTIVITY 6.3**
> Conduct the same activity as 6.2 with your own essays. Even without the use of the personal pronoun 'I' you should see yourself revealed in the essays and the choices you made, for example, your choice of essay topic, your choice of discipline, your choice of research papers, your choice of arguments.
> - Consider what do they reveal about you?

Activity 6.4 should also help to further illustrate the situatedness of other authors within their studies.

> **ACTIVITY 6.4**
> Again, using a journal that you are already familiar with read through a few of the articles and highlight where and how often the authors use the following phrases.
> - My/our intention ...
> - I/we argue ...
> - I/we demonstrate ...
> - My/our research approach ...
> - My/our method ...
> - Through my/our analysis ...
> - My/our argument is ...
> - Take a moment to reflect on what you can learn about the researcher's epistemological values and their views about a topic from how they use such phrases.
> - Having learnt about the researcher from their article do you still regard them as absent from their writing?

Activities 6.2, 6.3 and 6.4 begin to demonstrate how researchers, and that also includes you, unwittingly or on purpose, engage with and reveal themselves in their studies, sometimes regardless of the use of the word 'I'. We are clearly all embedded in what we write, we cannot escape it, nor perhaps should we want to. Traditionally, as Charmaz and Mitchel (1997: 194) have argued, silent authorship has been reassuringly cast as 'mature scholarship' and 'the proper voice is no voice at all'. However, as we shift our focus to the 'merit[s] in audible authorship' (Charmaz and Mitchel 1997: 194), we see how the 'I' of the author, rather than seen as a contaminating force, can provide a more varied and nuanced view, emphasizing our relationships with participants, our closeness to our work and our vulnerabilities. Plummer (2001: 180), now over twenty years ago, described a 'feminist-inspired' fight back 'reasserting the importance of *the self in the text*' (emphasis in the original), which bring us to the justification for the use of the word 'I'.

## Arguments for Using 'I'

Having outlined arguments that support the removal of the author from their text, we now focus on replacing or decentring the anonymous, distant and yet powerful third-person with the first-person self. Sanz (2011), amongst others, has argued that whilst the use of 'I' projects an image of the author in relation to their arguments, community and readers, many may choose to moderate their voice to comply with the perceived academic conventions in which their discipline sits. Similarly, Kuo (1999: 121) also regards written text as being an interaction between writer and reader, suggesting that the use of personal pronouns reveals the 'writer's perception of their own role in research and their relationship with expected readers'. Indeed, as we have previously explored, it can be argued that all writing carries an underlying 'palimpsest' about the uniqueness of the author (Spivak 1976: lxxvii). The use of personal projection, therefore, such as the inclusion of first-person pronouns can be considered authoritative instruments for self-representation (Ivanič 1998; Ivanič and Simpson 1992). Personal references can provide a clear indication to the reader of the perspective through which the author's arguments should be interpreted (Kuo 1999). Such use conveys the writer's convictions and can position the writer as an insider, holding categorical membership, within the academic community. Hyland (2001: 207) therefore argues that 'self-mention is ... a powerful rhetorical strategy for emphasising a writer's contribution'.

Cherry (1988) calls for a balance in the authoritative voice, thus representing oneself as both a proficient member of an academic discipline and offering personal qualities such as reliability and trustworthiness. This can particularly be the case in childhood studies, where researchers are often managing multiple agendas, such as the care and wellbeing of young participants, the responsibilities of the researcher and the salient issues that may arise from the topic. For example, Coombs and Richards (2023) in their research relating to children's perceptions of their play area, a repurposed graveyard, managed tensions between the assumed vulnerabilities of participants, sensitivity of the topic and the generation of data. Their account of this research, therefore, includes not only the presentation of data but reflexive discussions of researcher positionality.

In some disciplines, for example, the interdisciplinary field of disability studies, there is an explicit expectation that a researcher will demonstrate some form of insider knowledge by virtue of identifying as a disabled person or as being a family member or professional perhaps. This perspective is sufficiently dominant that when co-authoring a chapter regarding research with children with disabilities (Richards and Clark 2018), they felt it necessary to disclose that they did not identify as disabled, thus attempting to position themselves honestly and openly in this field. In so doing, readers and pertinently other disability scholars could determine the strength of their claims and knowledge, based not just on what they had said, but who they were.

Stapleton (2002: 177), however, claims that the 'case for voice ... has been overstated', and this can lead students 'into believing that expressions of identity take precedence over ideas and argumentation'. Nevertheless, as Woodiwiss, Smith and Lockwood (2017: x) argue, written narrative is 'a communicative event' with co-participants, the writer and the reader, where something is 'happening', intending to have a particular effect. Therefore, rather than just a representation of 'argumentation' as Stapleton suggests, text needs to be recognized as 'nuanced, situated and co-constitutive' (Woodiwiss, Smith and Lockwood 2017: x).

Within certain methodological approaches it is entirely consistent that the use of 'I' is available to the researcher as an instrumental tool to inform and highlight the interpretation of data, the situatedness of the researcher and the co-construction of data between participants and researcher. Ethnography, as we have seen, is one example where commonly participant observation, in which the researcher is embedded and active within the research context, is used. Here the researcher can actively build relationships (Vine 2018) with the participants or has already-existing relationships with them (Richards 2018). To attempt to distance these relationships and remove oneself from the narrative would be, not only, disingenuous but also counter-intuitive. The narrative turn in feminist research highlights the 'significance of identity, the subject, biography, the making of subjectivities and notions of interiority' (Woodiwiss, Smith and Lockwood 2017: viii). Thus, who is speaking is as important and relevant as what they are saying. From this perspective, authors construct themselves in their writing as actively as they build the arguments about the data they have produced. However, in contrast to positivist approaches where the presence of the researcher is unacknowledged, this process is fully and overtly recognized. Writing is clearly a particularly salient form of social action in the negotiation of identities as well as judging academic achievement (Hyland 2001). As Yilmaz (2013) claims, within qualitative approaches, the personal voice is evident through personal writing style, an engaging style of narrative and sometimes the use of the first-person pronoun.

As an anthropologist, Heather Montgomery spent considerable time researching with young prostitutes in Thailand. Her reflexive account, part of which is provided for you in activity 6.5, reveals not just the perspectives of her young participants but is also an excellent example of how the researcher can be revealed and present in the text. Montgomery does not shy away from this presence, but actively positions herself not only anthropologically but also personally in this article.

The excerpt provided represents the introduction to this article and is indicative of some of the points raised in this chapter so far.

### ACTIVITY 6.5

In this article I argue that in situations in which family relationships and ideas of filial duty are at odds with the researcher's understanding about what constitutes an appropriate adult relationship with children, analysis will inevitably be synonymous with an ethical dilemma. I confronted this conundrum while conducting ethnographic fieldwork between 1993 and 1994 among young prostitutes in a Thai slum community. I worked with children marginalized from conventional productive relations by their parents' experiences of unsuccessful economic migration to the outskirts of towns and cities, and who had to accommodate, early on, the burden of productive activity on which family livelihood and perpetuation of appropriate kin relations depended. Here, in the slums, conventional ideas about what constitutes legitimate productive activities were disrupted and the transition from a rural, village way of life to the town or city, and its different demands, had for most adults been largely unsuccessful. Their children, however, had found a way to make money from a particular form of prostitution involving client relations between both boys and girls and white, adult, males from the West. In this article I focus on children's own views and understandings of what their involvement with these 'clients' meant and I detail the ethical challenge that investigation and analysis of their perspective entail. I also look at how this affected the day-to-day life of an anthropologist in the field and what dilemmas and decisions this involved (Montgomery 2007: 415).

- Locate and read the full article ... Montgomery, H. (2007) 'Working with child prostitutes in Thailand: Problems of Practice and Interpretation', *Childhood*, 14(4), 415–30.

> - Identify examples where Montgomery reveals aspects of herself and write a short paragraph about what you now know about her.
> - Consider how persuasive Montgomery is in presenting her arguments and whether your position on any of the issues she raises has shifted because of this.
> - For further reflection on Montgomery's positionality, see … Montgomery, H. (2023) 'Owning our Mistakes: Confessions of an Unethical Researcher', in Richards, S. and Coombs, S. (Eds) Critical Perspectives on Research with Children: Reflexivity, Methodology and Researcher Identity, Bristol: Bristol University Press.

Having considered the ways in which Montgomery positions herself in her writing and in her research, you are now moving towards the point where you can begin to consider how you might emulate this style in, and throughout, your own dissertation. Begin by asking yourself when and how you might include yourself in your research, will you use the first-person pronoun, will you include personal details, or if not so overtly stated how might you acknowledge and reveal your presence in other, perhaps less explicit, ways. Importantly as Stanley and Wise (1993: 175, original emphasis) contend, 'the researcher is always and inevitably *in* the research'.

## Ways to Include 'Self' and 'I' in Your Research

Twenty years ago, Grbich (2004: 28) was arguing that the time was right for the quantitative scientific researcher of the past to become 'a more participatory being', one who could acknowledge the impact of self on the settings and findings of their research. At this time, she called for 'a heightened awareness of self in the process of knowledge creation' (Grbich 2004: 28–9) and suggested that 'as authority slips away, the dominant third-person voice of the author is replaced by the voices of participants, voices from other texts, or the "i"/"I" voice of the author speaking in her/his [their] own right' (Grbich 2004: 29).

Thus far, both sides of the argument, calling for either the inclusion or exclusion of the first-person pronoun in research, have been explored. The following sub-headings, however, will examine more closely, the ways in which you might incorporate yourself within and throughout the sections of your dissertation. Let us begin by saying that if you are embedded in a discipline, academic department or supervisory relationship, which eschews the use of 'I' for undergraduate or postgraduate level work, then the following considerations might act to facilitate your inclusion of self in more discreet and less obvious ways. Nevertheless, you will be present throughout your dissertation.

# Introduction

To start at the opening of your dissertation, the inclusion of 'self' can commence as soon as the introduction section to your study. This piece of writing opens the dialogue between you and your reader, it sets-the-scene for your project and justifies why the topic is important, relevant and interesting to you, and potentially your wider audience. Activity 6.6 provides you with an opportunity to begin your recognition and articulation of self in your own work.

---

**ACTIVITY 6.6**

Complete the following sentences to set in motion the recognition of yourself within your project.
- This topic is important to me because …
- My interest in this topic is influenced by …
- I feel the best way to explore this topic is … (theoretical, participatory, qualitatively, or quantitatively).
- How will I select my participants? Who will they be and why?
- What theories will I include?

---

Your consideration of activity 6.6 can help you appreciate that the decisions you make, and have already made, in relation to your study, are not only empirical but also personal. Each decision reveals something about you as a person and as a researcher. The uncovering and positioning of self begins with such statements and initiates the relationship between the author and the reader. By the end of the introduction, whether overtly stated or not, the reader will know several things about your topic, your relationship with this project and your epistemological choices. The dialogue between the reader and writer has begun.

## Review of the Literature

A literature review may seem a far cry from aspects of yourself, as it draws significantly upon the work of others. However, what you choose to include in your selected information, and what you equally choose to omit, says a great deal about you. Your literature review signals to your reader, your focus, interests and concerns, it affirms your imperative, and what you already deem important about this topic. How you position the literature to establish your claims and arguments illustrates your existing assumptions and ideas. A relationship begins to be established between your interests in the topic, demonstrated through your introduction, and the way in which you select and engage with salient literature, setting the scene for all subsequent arguments.

## Methodology and Methods

Just as you are deeply rooted in your research topic, you are also embedded in, and intimate with, the research approach you select. In some ways, your methodological approach might be chosen even before your topic choice, as your ideas align more readily with certain attitudes. For example, your research inclinations may have tendencies towards being qualitative or quantitative, objective or subjective, nomothetic or idiographic. Your adoption of a certain methodology, with its accompanying methods, may also be determined by your understanding of one approach above another, or the preference and expertise of your supervisor might be instrumental in your decisions.

When it comes to selecting methods for your research there are many, most of which combined with the methodologies in which they sit, allow for, even encourage, the presence of the researcher. Much of the research undertaken by childhood studies students, at any level, is broadly interpretivist, qualitative and often participatory. For instance, you might choose to run a focus group or conduct semi-structured interviews, you might elect to use visual methods such as drawings or photographs or you might facilitate role-playing or encourage the use of journal entries.

The choice of method and its deeper interrogation can be integral to revealing the researcher's self with, or without, the inclusion of 'I' in the text. It is often, so much more than preferring drawings to collages, diary entries to the collection of 'stuff', or small world play to asking children to design their 'ideal' play area. It can demonstrate just who a researcher is, their personality and emotions. The choice of method importantly highlights our own individual understanding and values in relation to children and childhood. We expose from within our methods, the tensions we may feel between children's agency and vulnerability, their so-called rights to participate or not, and the relevance of their voices.

## Ethics

All dissertations and research projects must have sections, which detail ethical issues and researcher's responses to them. These are often written in an abstract way where the researcher commits to established ethical guidelines, providing information to ensure informed consent, confidentiality and a right to withdraw. The conversations between the researcher and participants with regard to such things as right to withdraw or decisions about participation are often neglected or discounted within dissertation discussions. Yet they reveal the 'practice' of ethics and demonstrate how the researcher is 'doing' ethics. Therefore, an ethics section in a dissertation can move beyond the statements of ethical principles into examples of ethics in practice, and thus reveal you as the researcher through the decisions you make.

You may, for example, select or have selected the feminist principle of an ethic of care, which promotes nurturance, reciprocity and trust in research relationships. All of these require the researcher, as an individual, to be actively involved in developing those relationships. When exploring these principles in your research discussions you will inevitably be including aspects of yourself: when explaining how you upheld these ideas; why they were important; and the relationships that ensued. Despite any guiding principles you will find yourself making decisions in the field where you reveal yourself and your ethical values as a researcher, what Wall (2019) refers to as ethical moments. Montgomery (2023) in 'Confessions of an Unethical Researcher' reflexively explores and interrogates her ethical decisions and positionality. She reveals herself and her ethical values in this discussion, as you can by similar explorations of your own research decisions.

## Discussion

The discussion section of your dissertation normatively explores your data and findings but is also available to analyse the processes and challenges associated with data collection, and what you bring into the field. For example, an undergraduate student we supervised some years ago chose to give young children digital cameras, in order to photograph their educational landscapes. Different generational knowledge meant that half of the time allotted for the research was spent teaching the children to use these so-called simple devices. The consequence of this being the student lost valuable data collection time in the limited availability within the classroom schedule, and thus the student became anxious that she had insufficient data. Rather than simply confronting this experience as a field work failure, we encouraged the student to think reflexively about her experiences in the field, and the assumptions made by her, which influenced the events during the activity. We encouraged her to consider how her expectations about what would happen became explicit when something different happened, and furthermore how this revealed aspects self and her character in the data collection process. This reflexive discussion is worthy of inclusion in this section of a dissertation and speaks of assumptions we all have and bring with us into the research process. Whilst this is not a finding about children's perspectives of educational landscapes, it remains an important feature for discussion and can only be done successfully when we acknowledge ourselves in our research. When being reflexive in this way you are clearly bringing yourself, your assumptions and your knowledge into the field, and recognizing/acknowledging your influence. In the case above, the student could meaningfully explore all her presumptions and their direct impact on her data collection. Such vignettes therefore can become important discussions in a dissertation, where you are primarily focused on demonstrating your emerging knowledge of doing research.

## Self-Critical Review

In some dissertations it is possible to include a small summative section where you can reflect on your research journey. This is usually connected to the methodology chapter whereby conversations about your research values, which began there, can continue. Key components of your methodology can be interrogated and questioned, as well as your own experiences of using them in field work. For example, if you have highlighted the importance of reflexivity within your research project, the critical self-review can be a particularly useful space in which to be reflexive about your research encounters, possible unexpected data or incidents in the field. If, in your methodology section, you highlight the importance of children's voices and concepts such as agency, then it is here that you can evaluate these and what you have learnt in doing your own fieldwork. How easy or challenging were these methodological values to uphold? The critical self-review is normatively written in the past tense and from the first-person perspective, after all it is a reflexive account of your research experiences, which can demonstrate your critical knowledge and understanding of the research process.

With these discussions in mind, activity 6.7 provides a list, by no means exhaustive, which should set you thinking about your own key values and how you now regard them after doing research. These are valuable discussions to have in a self-critical review, where they can demonstrate a greater knowledge and understanding of research, its methods and your presence within it.

---

**ACTIVITY 6.7**

Using the themes highlighted below, write a few short sentences for each of these key methodological concepts, which may reflect your experiences in the field. Compare your experience of these with how they are promoted in textbooks. How straightforward were they to comply with, what issues, if any, were there?

- **Informed consent**: Is there such a thing as truly informed consent? Who gives it? Is it really children who do this?
- **The voices of children**: Whose voice are we hearing in the act of consent? What have you learnt about the voice of children? Is it as strong as you thought it would be? Whose voice is being brought to the forefront of research; is it the child's or your own as a researcher?
- **Child-led approach**: Can you look back and acknowledge that your study was really led by children or was it the adults leading?
- **Being ethical**: How ethical were you in practice?
- **Positionality**: What are your values around childhood? Were they acknowledged in your research, were they challenged? Were they changed?
- **Power relationships**: How powerful were you as a researcher? Did you feel powerful, or did you feel the children were more powerful? Was this power static or variable?
- **Interrogation of method**: Explore what you learnt about the efficacy or otherwise of your chosen method. Write a few sentences about how you found it in practice versus what the books said about it.

Students can often struggle with the self-critical review section of their dissertation. On occasion, it can be reduced to a rather dry discussion of how students met their research aims, or a sequential and mundane account of their research journey. Alternatively, we hope that activity 6.7 provides you with more useful content for this section. Indeed, having some of the conversations highlighted above enables you to successfully negotiate and extend the learning outcomes of your dissertation, and can provide greater insights into, and critical understanding of, your research.

## Conclusion

Writing in the first person can be constructed as contentious. Research approaches that privilege the values of objectivity and generalizability can resist the validity of the presence of the researcher, regarding it as a contamination to the field. However, this is not the whole story. As we have explored throughout this chapter, researchers reveal themselves implicitly in their research, whether they explicitly use 'I' or not. Whilst some approaches prefer to suppress the inclusion of self, others rely on and even celebrate an explicit presence. We have set out some of the varied positions on this contested issue, as we note that students can be confused about when, or whether, to include themselves in their discussions. As supervisors, we have often explained the presence, or absence, of 'I' for students across a range of levels. Our own perspective, which we believe is explicit, overt and unambiguous across our writing, arguments and claims within this volume, is that the researcher is inseparable from their research, and we should reflexively acknowledge this as a strength.

We have also set out ways in which you can include yourself, and therefore be present, in your own research, with or without, the use of the first-person pronoun. We hope such examples help you to recognize and account for yourself across all aspects of your dissertation, in your methodology, method, ethics, introduction, discussion and self-critical review. As a final activity in this volume, activity 6.8 asks you to review this chapter to consider the ways in which we, as authors, are present here, and your feelings towards the value of our company. Finally, we encourage you to experiment with your own academic writing by using your personal voice, requesting feedback on it from your supervisors, and thus be better informed about the ways in which you have, as an individual, influenced your research.

---

**ACTIVITY 6.8**

As a final activity, we would like you to utilize this chapter by responding to the requests below.

- Make notes of where we have brought ourselves into the text, perhaps by claiming an argument, self-referencing or simply using 'I' or 'we'.
- Consider how effective this has been in persuading you to our viewpoint.
- Perhaps explore the debates we have presented in this chapter with your supervisor. If you then go on to write from a more subjective, self-conscious perspective, our efforts have been successful.

# REFERENCES

Abell, J., Locke, A., Condor, S., Gibson, S. and Stevenson, C. (2006), 'Trying Similarity, Doing Difference: The Role of Interviewer Self-Disclosure in Interview Talk with Young People', *Qualitative Research*, 6(2), 221–44.

Alanen, L. (1988), 'Rethinking Childhood', *Acta Sociologica*, 31(1), 53–67. https://doi.org/10.1177/000169938803100105.

Altheide, D. and Johnson, J. (1994), 'Criteria for Assessing Interpretive Validity in Qualitative Research', in Denzin, N. and Lincoln, Y. (eds), *Handbook of Qualitative Research*, 485–99, Thousand Oaks, CA: Sage.

Arnaudet, M. L. and Barrett, M. E. (1984), *Approaches to Academic Reading and Writing*, Englewood Cliffs, NJ: Prentice-Hall.

Atkinson, P. and Coffey, A. (2003), 'Revisiting the Relationship between Participant Observation and Interviewing', in Gubrium, J. F. and Holstein, J. A. (eds), *Postmodern Interviewing*, 109–22, London: Sage.

Back, L. (2007), *The Art of Listening*, Oxford, New York: Berg.

Baker, C. D. (2003), 'Ethnomethodological Analyses of Interviews', in Holstein, J. A. and Gubrium, J. F. (eds), *Inside Interviewing: New Lenses New Concerns*, 395–412, London: Sage.

Beauchamp, T. L. and Childress, J. F. ([1979] 2019), *Principles of Biomedical Ethics*, 8th Edition, New York: Oxford University Press.

Becker, H. S. (1967), 'Whose Side Are We On?' *Social Problems*, 14(3), 239–47. https://doi.org/10.2307/799147.

Bhatt, C. (2012), 'Doing a Dissertation', in Seale, C. (ed), *Researching Society and Culture*, 3rd Edition, 153–78, London: Sage.

Biber, D. and Gray, B. (2010), 'Challenging Stereotypes about Academic Writing: Complexity, Elaboration, Explicitness', *Journal of English for Academic Purposes*, 9(1), 2–20.

Boggis, A. (2011), 'Deafening Silences: Researching with Inarticulate Children', *Disability Studies Quarterly*, 31(4). https://doi.org/10.18061/dsq.v31i4.1710.

Borbasi, S., Jackson, D. and Wilkes, L. (2005), 'Fieldwork in Nursing Research: Positionality, Practicalities and Predicaments', *Journal of Advanced Nursing*, 5(5), 493–501.

Brown, C., Spiro, J. and Quinton, S. (2020), 'The Role of Research Ethics Committees: Friend or Foe in Educational Research? An Exploratory Study', *British Educational Research Journal*, 46(4), 747–69.

Burman, E. (2008), *Deconstructing Developmental Psychology*, 2nd Edition, London: Routledge.

Cadman, K. (1997), 'Thesis Writing for International Students: A Question of Identity?' *English for Specific Purposes*, 16(1), 3-14.

Canosa, A. and Graham, A. (2020), 'Tracing the Contribution of Childhood Studies: Maintaining Momentum while Navigating Tensions', *Childhood*, 27(1), 25-7.

Canosa, A., Graham, A. and Wilson, E. (2018), 'Reflexivity and Ethical Mindfulness in Participatory Research with Children: What Does It Really Look Like?' *Childhood*, 25(3), 400-15.

Chang, Y. and Swales, J. (1999), 'Informal Elements in English Academic Writing: Threats or Opportunities for Advanced Non-native Speakers', in Candlin, C. N. and Hyland, K. (eds), *Writing: Texts, Processes and Practices*, 145-67, London: Longman.

Charmaz, K. and Mitchell, R. (1997), 'The Myth of Silent Authorship: Self, Substance, and Style in Ethnographic Writing', in Hertz, R. (ed), *Reflexivity and Voice*, 193-215, London: Sage.

Cheney, K. (2011), 'Children as Ethnographers: Reflections on the Importance of Participatory Research in Assessing Orphans Needs', *Childhood*, 18(2), 166-79.

Cherry, R. D. (1988), 'Ethos versus Persona: Self-Representation in Written Discourse', *Written Communication*, 5(3), 251-76. https://doi.org/10.1177/0741088388005003001.

Chiseri-Strater, E. (1996), 'Turning in upon Ourselves: Positionality, Subjectivity and Reflexivity in Case Study and Ethnographic Research', in Mortensen, P. and Kirsch, G. E. (eds), *Ethics and Representation in Qualitative Studies of Literacy*, 115-32, 1111 W. Kenyon Road, Urbana, IL: National Council of Teachers of English.

Christiansen, P. H. (2004), 'Children's Participation in Ethnographic Research: Issues of Power and Representation', *Children and Society*, 18(2), 165-76.

Clark, J. and Richards, S. (2017), 'The Cherished Conceits of Research with Children: Does Seeking the Agentic Voice of the Child through Participatory Methods Deliver What It Promises', in Castro, I. E., Swauger, M. and Harger, B. (eds), *Researching Children and Youth: Methodological Issues, Strategies, and Innovations*, Sociological Studies of Children and Youth Volume 22, 127-47, Bingley: Emerald Publishing.

Coffey, A. (1999), *The Ethnographic Self: Fieldwork and the Representation of Reality*, London: Sage.

Cohen, L., Manion, L. and Morrison, L. (2011), *Research Methods in Education*, Abingdon: Routledge.

Coombs, S. (2014), 'Death Wears a T-Shirt: Listening to Young People Talk about Death', *Mortality*, 19(3), 284-302.

Coombs, S. (2017), *Young People's Perspectives on End-of-Life: Death, Culture and the Everyday*, Cham, Switzerland: Palgrave Macmillan.

Coombs, S. and Richards, S. (2023), 'A Bump on the Head in the Graveyard: Palimpsests of Death, Selves, Care and Touch', in Richards, S. and Coombs, S. (eds), *Critical Perspectives on Research with Children: Reflexivity, Methodology and Researcher Identity*, 138-56, Bristol: Bristol University Press.

Cooper, V. (2023), 'Child Focused Research: Disconnected and Disembodied Voices', *Childhood*, 30(1), 71-85. https://doi.org/10.1177/09075682221132084.

Corsaro (1997), *Sociology of Childhood*, London: Sage.

de Laine, M. (1997), *Ethnography: Theory and Applications in Health Research*, Sydney: MacLennan & Petty.

Denzin, N. K. (1986), *Interpretive Biography*, Newbury Park, CA: Sage.

Denzin, N. and Lincoln, Y. (2008) (eds), *The Landscape of Qualitative Research*, London: Sage.

Dickson-Swift, V., James, E. L. and Liamputtong, P. (2008), *Undertaking Sensitive Research in the Health and Social Sciences: Managing Boundaries, Emotions and Risk*, Cambridge: Cambridge University Press.

Dunbar, C., Rodriques, D. and Parker, L. (2002), 'Race, Subjectivity, and the Interview Process', in Gubrium, J. F. and Holstein, J. A. (eds), *Handbook of Interview Research*, 279–98, Thousand Oaks, CA: Sage.

Dutton, H., Deanne, K. L. and Bullen, P. (2022), 'Exploring the Benefits and Risks of Mentor Self-Disclosure: Relationship Quality and Ethics in Youth Mentoring', *Kotuitui: New Zealand Journal of Social Sciences Online*, 22(1), 116–33.

Eder, D. and Fingerson, L. (2003), 'Interviewing Children and Adolescents', in Holstein, J. A. and Gubrium, J. F. (eds), *Inside Interviewing: New Lenses, New Concerns*, 33–53, London: Sage.

Einstein, A. (1934), *Essays in Science*, New York: The Philosophical Library.

Ethical Research Involving Children (ERIC 2019), available at https://childethics.com [Accessed on 26 February 2024].

Fine, M. (1994), 'Working the Hyphens: Reinventing Self and Other in Qualitative Research', in Denzin, N. K. and Lincoln, Y. S. (eds), *Handbook of Qualitative Research*, 70–82, Thousand Oaks, CA: Sage.

Foucault, M. (1972), *The Archaeology of Knowledge*, trans Sheridan Smith, A. M., New York: Pantheon Books.

Gallacher, L.-A. and Gallagher, M. (2008), 'Methodological Immaturity in Childhood Research? Thinking through "Participatory Methods"', *Childhood*, 15(4), 499–516. https://doi.org/10.1177/0907568208091672.

Garfinkel, H. (1967), *Studies in Ethnomethodology*, Englewood Cliffs, NJ: Prentice-Hall.

Geertz, G. (1973), *Thick Description: Towards an Interpretive Theory of Culture; Selected Essays*, New York: Basic Books.

Goodley, D. and Runswick-Cole, R. (2016), 'Becoming Dishuman: Thinking about the Human through Dis/Ability', *Discourse: Studies in the Cultural Politics of Education*, 37(1), 1–15.

Grbich, C. (2004), *New Approaches in Social Research*, London: Sage.

Greenbank, P. (2003), 'The Role of Values in Educational Research: The Case for Reflexivity', *British Educational Research Journal*, 26(6), 791–801.

Gubrium, J. and Holstein, J. (1999), 'At the Border of Narrative and Ethnography', *Journal of Contemporary Ethnography*, 28(5), 561–73.

Hacking, I. (1986), 'Making up People', in Heller, P., Sosna, M. and Wellberry, D. (eds), *Reconstructing Individualism*, 222–36, Stanford, CA: Stanford University Press.

Hall, S., Critcher, C., Jefferson, T., Clarke, J. and Roberts, B. (1978), *Policing the Crisis: Mugging, the State, and Law and Order*, London and Basingstoke: The Macmillan Press.

Hallett, C. and Prout, A. (2003) (eds), *Hearing the Voices of Children: Social Policy for a New Century*, London: Routledge.

Hammersley, M. (2015), 'Research Ethics and the Concept of Children's Rights', *Children and Society*, 29(6), 569–82.

Hammersley, M. and Atkinson, P. (1995), *Ethnography Principles in Practice*, 2nd Edition, London: Routledge.

Hart, R. (1992), 'Children's Participation: From Tokenism to Citizenship', *Innocenti Essays No.4*, UNICEF (online), available at https://www.unicef-irc.org/publications/100-childrens-participation-from-tokenism-to-citizenship.html [Accessed on 5 March 2023].

Hart, N. and Crawford-Wright, A. (1999), 'Research as Therapy, Therapy as Research: Ethical Dilemmas in New-Paradigm Research', *British Journal of Guidance & Counselling*, 27(2), 205–14. https://doi.org/10.1080/03069889908256265.

Hebdige, D. (1979), *Subculture: The Meaning of Style*, London: Routledge.

Hesse-Biber, S. H. and Leavy, P. (2011), *The Practice of Qualitative Research*, 2nd Edition, Los Angeles, CA: Sage.

Holstein, J. A. and Gubrium, J. F. (1995), *The Active Interview*, Thousand Oaks, CA: Sage.

Horgan, D. (2017), 'Child Participatory Research Methods: Attempts to Go Deeper', *Childhood*, 24(2), 245–59.

Howarth, C. (2002), 'Using the Theory of Social Representations to Explore Difference in the Research Relationship', *Qualitative Research*, 2(1), 21–34.

Hydén, M. (2008), 'Narrating Sensitive Topics', in Andrews, M., Squire, C. and Tamboukou, M. (eds), *Doing Narrative Research*, 122–136, London: Sage.

Hyland, K. (2001), 'Humble Servants of the Discipline? Self-Mention in Research Articles', *English for Specific Purposes*, 20(3), 207–26.

Isaacs, T. (2002), 'Feminism and Agency', *Canadian Journal of Philosophy*, Supplementary Volume 28, 129–54.

Ivanič, R. (1998), *Writing and Identity: The Discoursal Construction of Identity in Academic Writing*, Amsterdam: John Benjamin Publishing Company.

Ivanič, R. and Simpson, J. (1992) 'Who's Who in Academic Writing', in Fairclough, N. (ed), *Critical Language Awareness*, 141–73, London: Routledge.

Jackson, A. Y. and Mazzei, L. A. (2008), 'Experience and "I" in Autoethnography: A Deconstruction', *International Review of Qualitative Research*, 1(3), 299–318. https://doi.org/10.1525/irqr.2008.1.3.299.

James, A. and Prout, A. (1997) (eds), *Constructing and Reconstructing Childhood: Contemporary Issues in the Sociological Study of Children*, 2nd Edition, London: Falmer.

James, A., Jenks, C. and Prout, A. (1998), *Theorizing Childhood*, Cambridge: Polity Press.

Jordan, A. B. (2006), 'Make Yourself at Home: The Social Construction of Research Roles in Family Studies', *Qualitative Research*, 6(2), 169–85.

Jenks, C. (1996), *Childhood*, London: Routledge.

Kuo, C. H. (1999), 'The Use of Personal Pronouns: Role Relationships in Scientific Journal Articles', *English for Specific Purposes*, 18(2), 121–38.

Lachowicz, D. (1981), 'On the Use of the Passive Voice for Objectivity, Author Responsibility and Dodging in EST', *Science of Science*, 2(6), 105–15.

Lahman, M. K. E. (2008), 'Always Othered: Ethical Research with Children', *Journal of Early Childhood Research*, 6(3), 281–300.

Lerner, M. J. (1980), *The Belief in a Just World: A Fundamental Delusion*, New York/London: Plenum.

Lester, J. D. (1993), *Writing Research Papers*, 7th Edition, New York: Harper Collins.

Liamputtong, P. (2007), *Researching the Vulnerable*, London: Sage.

Lipson, J. (1989), 'The Use of Self in Ethnographic Research', in Morse, J. (ed) *Qualitative Nursing Research: A Contemporary Dialogue*, 61–75, Rockville, MD: Aspen Publications.

Lyttle Storrod, M. (2023), 'Do No Online Harm: Balancing Safeguarding with Researchers and Participants in Online Research with Sensitive Populations', in Richards, S. and Coombs, S. (eds), *Critical Perspectives in Research with Children: Reflexivity, Methodology and Researcher Identity*, 10–28, Bristol: Bristol University Press.

Madden, R. (2010), *Being Ethnographic*, London: Sage.

Martins, P. C., Oliveira, V. H. and Tendais, I. (2018), 'Research with Children and Young People on Sensitive Topics: The Case of Poverty and Delinquency', *Childhood*, 25(4), 458–72.

Mauthner, N. S. and Doucet, A. (2003), 'Reflexive Accounts and Accounts of Reflexivity in Qualitative Data Analysis', *Sociology*, 37(3), 413–31.

Mayall, B. (2002), *Towards a Sociology for Childhood: Thinking from Children's Lives*, Buckingham: Open University Press.

Mayes, E. (2019), 'The Mis/Uses of "Voice" in (Post)Qualitative Research with Children and Young People: Histories, Politics and Ethics', *International Journal of Qualitative Research in Education Studies*, 32(10), 1191–209.

McCrostie, J. (2008), 'Writer Visibility in EFL Learner Academic Writing: A Corpus-Based Study', *ICAME Journal*, 32, 97–114.

McTague, T., Froyum, C. and Risman, B. J. (2017), 'Learning about Inequality from Kids: Interviewing Strategies for Getting Beneath Equality Rhetoric', in Castro, I. E., Swauger, M. and Harger, B. (eds), *Researching Children and Youth: Methodological Issues, Strategies, and Innovations*, Sociological Studies of Children and Youth Volume 22, 277–301, Bingley: Emerald Publishing.

Miller, J. and Glassner, B. (1997) 'The Inside and the Outside: Finding Realities in Interviews', in Silverman, D. (ed), *Qualitative Research: Theory, Method and Practice*, 99–112, London: Sage.

Montgomery, H. (2007), 'Working with Child Prostitutes in Thailand: Problems of Practice and Interpretation', *Childhood*, 14(4), 415–30.

Montgomery, H. (2023), 'Owning Our Mistakes: Confessions of an Unethical Researcher', in Richards, S and Coombs, S. (eds), *Critical Perspectives on Research with Children: Reflexivity, Methodology and Researcher Identity*, 157–71, Bristol: Bristol University Press.

Oakes, P. J., Haslam, S. A. and Turner, J. C. (1994), *Stereotyping and Social Reality*, Oxford: Basil Blackwell.

Oakley, A. (1981), 'Interviewing Women: A Contradiction in Terms?' in Roberts, H. (ed), *Doing Feminist Research*, 30–61, London: Routledge.

Perelman, C. (1963), *The Idea of Justice and the Problem of Argument*, London: Routledge Kegan Paul.

Petch-Tyson, S. (1998), 'Writer/Reader Visibility in EFL Written Discourse', in Granger, S. (ed), *Learner English on Computer*, 107–18, London: Routledge.

Philo, C. (2011), 'Foucault, Sexuality and When Not to Listen to Children', *Children's Geographies*, 9(2), 123–27.

Plummer, K. (2001), *Documents of Life 2: An Invitation to a Critical Humanism*, London: Sage.

Plummer, K. (2008), 'Critical Humanism and Queer Theory: Living with the Tensions', in Denzin, N. and Lincoln, S. (eds), *The Landscape of Qualitative Research*, 3rd Edition, 477–99, London: Sage.

Poindexter, C. C. (2003), 'The Ubiquity of Ambiguity in Research Interviewing: An Exemplar', *Qualitative Social Work*, 2(4), 383–409.

Potter, J. and Wetherell, M. (1987), *Discourse and Social Psychology: Beyond Attitudes and Behaviour*, London: Sage.

Powell, M. A., Graham, A., McArthur, M., Moore, T., Chalmers, J. and Taplin, S. (2019), 'Children's Participation in Research on Sensitive Topics: Addressing Concerns of Decision-Makers', *Children's Geographies*, 18(3), 325–38.

Powell, M. A., Graham, A., McArthur, M., Moore, T., Chalmers, J. and Taplin, S. (2020), 'Children's Participation in Research on Sensitive Topics: Addressing Concerns of Decision-Makers', *Children's Geographies*, 18(3), 328–38.

Prout, A. (2005), *The Future of Childhood: Towards the Interdisciplinary Study of Children*, Abingdon: RoutledgeFalmer.

Punch, S. (2002), 'Research with Children: The Same or Different from Research with Adults?' *Childhood*, 9(3), 321–41.

Raby, R. (2014), 'Children's Participation as Neo-Liberal Governance?' *Discourse: Studies in the Cultural Politics of Education*, 35(1), 77–89.

Rawat, A. (2023), 'Researching Children's Experiences in a Conflict Zone and a Red-Light Area: Conducting Ethnographic Fieldwork in India and Kashmir', in Richards, S. and Coombs, S. (eds), *Critical Perspectives on Research with Children: Reflexivity, Methodology and Researcher Identity*, 63–81, Bristol: Bristol University Press.

Reinharz, S. (1997), 'Who Am I? The Need for a Variety of Selves in the Field', in Hertz, R. (ed), *Reflexivity and Voice*, 3–20, Thousand Oaks, CA: Sage.

Richards, S. (2012), 'What the Map Cuts Up the Story Cuts Across: Narratives of Belonging in Intercountry Adoption', *Adoption and Fostering*, 36(3), 104–11.

Richards, S. (2013), 'Stories of Paper and Blood: Narratives of Belonging in Families of Daughters Adopted from China', PhD Dissertation, Institute of Education: University College London.

Richards, S. (2018), 'Chóng ér fēi: Cultural Performances of Belonging in Intercountry Adoptive Families', in Vine, T., Clark, J., Richards, S. and Weir, D. (eds), *Ethnographic Research and Analysis: Anxiety, Identity and Self*, 53–76, London: Palgrave Macmillan.

Richards, S. and Clark, J. (2018), 'Research with Disabled Children: Tracing the Past, Present, and Future', in Boggis, A. (ed), *Dis/Abled Childhoods? A Transdisciplinary Approach*, 187–209, Hampshire: Palgrave Macmillan.

Richards, S. and Coombs, S. (2023) (eds), *Critical Perspectives on Research with Children: Reflexivity, Methodology and Researcher Identity*, Bristol: Bristol University Press.

Richards, S., Clark, J. and Boggis, A. (2015), *Ethical Research with Children: Untold Narratives and Taboos*, Basingstoke: Palgrave Macmillan.

Riessman, C. K. (1994), 'Subjectivity Matters: The Positioned Investigator', in Riessman, C. K. (ed), *Qualitative Studies in Social Work Research*, 139–52, Thousand Oaks: Sage.

Ristock, J. L. and Pennell, J. (1996), *Community Research as Empowerment: Feminist Links, Postmodern Interruptions*, Toronto: Oxford University Press.

Roberts, H. (2008), 'Listening to Children: And Hearing Them', in Christensen, P. and James, A. (eds), *Research with Children: Perspectives and Practices*, 2nd Edition, 260–75, Abingdon: Routledge.

Ryan-Flood, R. and Gill, R. (2010) (eds), *Secrecy and Silence in the Research Process: Feminist Reflections*, London: Routledge.

Sanchez Taylor, J. and O'Connell Davidson, J. (2010), 'Unknowable Secrets and Golden Silence: Reflexivity and Research on Sex Tourism', in Ryan-Flood, R. and Gill, R. (eds), *Secrecy and Silence in the Research Process: Feminist Reflections*, 42–53, London: Routledge.

Sanz, R. S. (2011), 'The Construction of the Author's Voice in Academic Writing: The Interplay of Cultural and Disciplinary Factors', *Text & Talk: An Interdisciplinary Journal of Language Discourse Communication Studies*, 31(2), 173–93. https://doi.org/10.1515/text.2011.008.

Savin-Baden, M. and Howell Major, C. (2013), *Qualitative Research: The Essential Guide to Theory and Practice*, Abingdon: Routledge.

Shakespeare, T. (2006), *Disability Rights and Wrongs*, London: Routledge.

Shiraani, F., Shaheer, I. and Carr, N. (2022), 'Procedural Ethics vs Being Ethical: A Critical Appraisal', in Okumus, F., Rasoolimanesh, S. M. and Jahani, S. (eds), *Contemporary Research Methods in Hospitality and Tourism*, 21–37, Bingley: Emerald Publishing.

Silverman, D. (1993), *Interpreting Qualitative Data: Methods for Analysing Talk, Text and Interaction*, London: Sage.

Sinha, P. (2023), 'Responding Reflexively, Relationally, and Reciprocally to Unequal Childhoods', in Richards, S. and Coombs, S. (eds), *Critical Perspectives on Research with Children: Reflexivity, Methodology and Researcher Identity*, 42–62, Bristol: Bristol University Press.

Spivak, G. C. (1976), 'Translator's Preface', in Derrida, J. (ed), *Of Grammatology*, lxxvii, Baltimore, MD: Johns Hopkins University Press.

Spyrou, S. (2011), 'The Limits of Children's Voices: From Authenticity to Critical, Reflexive Representation', *Childhood*, 18(2), 151–65.

Stanley, L. and Wise, S. (1993), *Breaking out Again: Feminist Ontology and Epistemology*, London: Routledge.

Stapleton, P. (2002), 'Critiquing Voice as a Viable Pedagogical Tool in L2 Writing', *Journal of Second Language Writing*, 11(3), 177–90. 10.1016/S1060-3743(02)00070-X.

Stella, M. and Boggis, A. (2023), 'Capturing Narratives: Adopting a Reflexive Approach to Research with Disabled Young People', in Richards, S. and Coombs, S. (eds), *Critical Perspectives on Research with Children: Reflexivity, Methodology and Researcher Identity*, 82–95, Bristol: Bristol University Press.

Sullivan, D. L. (1996), 'Displaying Disciplinarity', *Written Communication*, 13(2), 221–50. https://doi.org/10.1177/0741088396013002003.

Taylor, J. (2011), 'The Intimate Insider: Negotiating the Ethics of Friendship When Doing Insider Research', *Qualitative Research*, 11(3), 3–22.

Thomas, G. (2013), *How to Do Your Research Project: A Guide for Students in Education and Applied Social Sciences*, 2nd Edition, London: Sage.

Tong, R. (1999) 'Feminist Philosophy', in Audi, R. (Ed), *The Cambridge Dictionary of Philosophy*, 2nd Edition, 305–307, New York: Cambridge University Press.

Tronto, J. C. ([1993] 2009), *Moral Boundaries: A Political Argument for an Ethic of Care*, New York: Routledge.

Tyrell, K. (2023), 'Youth Social Action: Shaping Communities, Driving Change', in Richards, S. and Coombs, S. (eds), *Critical Perspectives on Research with Children: Reflexivity, Methodology and Researcher Identity*, 96–115, Bristol: Bristol University Press.

United Nations Convention on the Rights of the Child (1989), UNICEF (online), available at https://www.unicef.org.uk/wp-content/uploads/2016/08/unicef-convention-rights-child-uncrc.pdf [Accessed on 13 September 2023].

Uprichard, E. (2010), 'Questioning Research with Children: Discrepancy between Theory and Practice?' *Children and Society*, 24(1), 3–13.

Van Maanen, J., Manning, J. P. and Miller, M. (1989), 'Editors Introduction', in Hunt, J. C. (ed), *Psychoanalytic Aspects of Fieldwork*, Qualitative Research Methods, Series. 18, 5–6, Beverley Hills, CA: Sage.

Vine, T. (2018), 'Methodology: From Paradigms to Paradox', in Vine, T., Clark, J., Richards, S. and Weir, D. (eds), *Ethnographic Research and Analysis: Anxiety, Identity and Self*, 273–300, London: Palgrave Macmillan.

Wall, J. (2010), *Ethics in the Light of Childhood*, Washington, DC: Georgetown University Press.

Wall, J. (2019): 'From Childhood Studies to Childism: Reconstructing the Scholarly and Social Imaginations', *Children's Geographies*, 20(3), 257–270. DOI: 10.1080/14733285.2019.166891 [Accessed 11 May 2024].

Wenzal, M. (2000), 'Justice and Identity the Significance of Inclusion and the Justice Motive', *Personality and Social Psychology*, 26(2), 57–176.

Woodiwiss, J., Smith, K. and Lockwood, K. (2017) (eds), 'Preface: Telling Lives in Feminist Narrative Inquiry'*Feminist Narrative Research: Opportunities and Challenges*, vii–xvii, London: Palgrave Macmillan.

Yilmaz, K. (2013), 'Comparison of Quantitative and Qualitative Research Traditions: Epistemological, Theoretical, and Methodological Differences', *European Journal of Education*, 48(2), 311–25. https://doi.org/10.1111/ejed.12014.

Zignon, J. (2008), *Mortality: An Anthropological Perspective*, Oxford: Berg.

Zonio, H. (2017), '"Is That a Mom and Dad Church?" Children's Constructions of Meaning through Focus Group Interviews', in Castro, I. E., Swauger, M. and Harger, B. (eds), *Researching Children and Youth: Methodological Issues, Strategies, and Innovations*, 251–73, Bingley: Emerald Publishing.

# INDEX

Abell, J. 93, 95
agency in child-centred research 66–9
Altheide, D. 83
Atkinson, P. 80, 84

Back, L., *The Art of Listening* 102–3
Baker, C. D. 80
Beauchamp, T. L. 15
Bhatt, C. 43
Biber, D. 121
Boggis, A. 20, 65
Brown, C. 17
Bullen, P. 95
Burman, E. 59

Cadman, K. 124
Canosa, A. 46, 72
category membership and entitlement
   assigned attributes 88
   cultural competence 89
   positioning 91
   public acknowledgement 92
   recruitment strategy 90
   selected topic 89
   social categorization 87
Chang, Y. 123
Charmaz, K. 121, 127
Cherry, R. D. 128
child-centred research 2–3, 7–8, 66–9
   contextual details (voice, agency and participation) 73–4
   continuum of 61–3
   participation 69–73
   rise of 58–61
   voice 64–6
childhood and links, methodology 44–6
Childress, J. F. 15
Chiseri-Strater, E. 82

Clark, J. 20, 65, 69
code of conduct 29
Coffey, A. 87
continuum of child-centred research 61–3
Coombs, S. 71–2, 130
Cooper, V. 64
creative interviewing 93
critical self-review 98, 136–38

data collection 8–9, 94, 105–9
   extraneous 9, 116–17
   planning 102–5
   recognizing 109–11
   silence, students 114–15
   unexpected data 111–16
Deanne, K. L. 95
Denzin, N. K. 58, 83, 115
Dickson-Swift, V. 51, 77, 79
dilemmas 20, 38, 102, 109
   ethical 3, 34–5, 61, 96, 113, 130
disability studies 59, 66, 128
Disclosure and Barring Service (DBS) 19, 25
dissertation 2, 11–12, 36–7, 68, 134–38. *See also* data collection; methodology
   concepts, application of 97–8
   supervision 101, 106, 123–4
documentation
   approval 28
   DBS 25
   information letters and consent 26–7
   recruitment strategy 25–6
   research proposal 24–5
   research schedule 26
Dunbar, C. 94
Dutton, H. 97

# INDEX

Einstein, A. 123
Ethical Research Involving Children (ERIC) 28–9
ethic of care 30–1
ethics in research with children 4–5
   committee responsibilities 19–20
   decision-making 15–16
   description 14
   dissertation 36–7
   documentation 24–8
   (un)ethical vignettes 15, 31–5
   history 16
   human participants, lack of 35–6
   and morality 14–15
   principles and practice 28–31
   procedures and approval 17–20
   'self' and 'I' 131–2, 134
   topic choice 20–3

feminism 30, 51–2, 66
Fine, M. 82
first-person pronoun in academic writing 9–12
   arguments against 121–7
   arguments for 127–31
   ways to include 131–2

Gallacher, L.-A. 102
Gallagher, M. 102
Gill, R. 79
Graham, A. 46, 72
Gray, B. 121
Grbich, C. 28, 78–9, 131
Gubrium, J. F. 83, 92

Hacking, I. 88
Hammersley, M. 80, 84
Hart, R. 62
   ladder of participation 61
Hesse-Biber, S. H. 36, 43, 50
Holstein, J. A. 83, 92
Horgan, D. 17, 63
Howarth, C. 91
Hydén, M. 22
Hyland, K. 119, 121, 125, 128

information letters and consent 26–7
interpretivism 6, 49–50
Isaacs, T. 66

Jackson, A. Y. 120
James, A. 44, 59
James, E. L. 51, 77, 79
Jenks, C. 59
Johnson, J. 83
Jordan, A. B. 94

Kuo, C. H. 127

Lachowicz, D. 122
Lahman, M. K. E. 46
Leavy, P. 36, 43, 50
Lerner, M. J. 91
Lester, J. D. 122
Liamputtong, P. 51, 77, 79
Lincoln, Y. 58, 115
Lipson, J. 84

Martins, P. C. 22
Mayall, B. 60
Mayes, E. 64–5
Mazzei, L. A. 120
McCrostie, J. 121
methodology 6–7
   analogy 41–2
   childhood and links to 44–6
   construct 46–8
   definition 43
   features 48–52
   and me 52–3
   our/your research 53–4
Milgram, S. 15
Mitchell, R. 121, 127
Montgomery, H. 113, 129, 130
   Confessions of an Unethical Researcher 135

Oliveira, V. H. 22
our/your research methodology 53–4

palimpsest 120, 127
Parker, L. 92
participation of children, research 69–73
Pennell, J. 80
Petch-Tyson, S. 123–4
Plummer, K. 29, 122, 127
Poindexter, C. C. 82
positionality, qualitative research
   category membership 85–6
   definition 82
   relationships 83–4
   selves, fieldwork 83, 85
positivist methodology 48–9
Potter, J. 87
power relations in research 34
procedures and approval 17–20
Prout, A. 44, 59, 60

qualitative research 8, 50–1, 82–6
   category membership and entitlement 87–92
   to dissertation 97–8
   self-disclosure 92–4
   subjectivity and reflexivity 77–82
Quinton, S. 17

raison d'etre 64, 69
realism 49
reflexivity in qualitative research 35, 80, 84
   interview 81–2
   knowledge production 79
   objectivity 82
   transformative 85
Reinharz, S. 36, 85, 93
relativism 50
research relationships 3, 57, 75–6, 83–4, 107, 135
Richards, S. 20, 65, 69, 72, 84, 128
Ristock, J. L. 80
Rodriques, D. 92
Ryan-Flood, R. 79

Sanz, R. S. 127
'self' and 'I' in research
   discussion section, dissertation 135–6
   ethics 134–5
   literature review 133
   methodology and methods 133–4
   self-critical review 136–8
self-disclosure in research
   fear of contamination 92
   limitations of 95–7
   relationship building 92–3
silent authorship 120, 127
Silverman, D. 82
Spiro, J. 17
Spivak, G. C. 120
Spyrou, S. 64
Stapleton, P. 128–9
subjectivity in qualitative research
   description 77
   openness 79
   and researchers presence, work 78
Sullivan, D. L. 125
Swales, J. 123
symbolic interactionism 58–9
systematic checking of ethics 17–18

Tendais, I. 22
Thomas, G. 17, 49
topic sensitivity 20–3

United Nations Convention on the Rights of the Child (1989) 57
Untreated Syphilis Study at Tuskegee (USPHS) 15
Uprichard, E. 70

voice, child-centred research 64–6

Wall, J. 30, 135
Wetherell, M. 87
Wilson, E. 72
written narrative 128–9

Yilmaz, K. 124, 129